The Unique Party-Cookbook You've Been Waiting For!

Now you can entertain at home with grace and flair! *Woman's Day® Complete Guide to Entertaining,* by one of America's most trusted authorities on cooking and hostessing, is full of delicious, easy-to-prepare recipes and menus for casual get-togethers or formal dinner parties. Every gathering, from a brunch to a barbeque, is fully covered in separate sections. Hostesses who entertain often will find exciting ideas for sensational new dishes—and the beginning hostess will discover the ease and joy of at-home entertaining!

Here's a sample menu, from the perfect book for *every* hostess:

DINNER PARTY

Quick Seafood Bisque
Parsley-Stuffed
Cornish Game Hens
Peas with Mushrooms
Grilled Herb Tomatoes
Oven-Braised Potatoes
Apricot-Orange Cream

Woman's Day®

Complete Guide to Entertaining

Carol Cutler

PUBLISHED BY POCKET BOOKS NEW YORK

Another *Original* publication of POCKET BOOKS

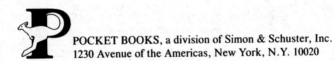 POCKET BOOKS, a division of Simon & Schuster, Inc.
1230 Avenue of the Americas, New York, N.Y. 10020

ISBN: 0-671-44671-1

First Pocket Books trade paperback printing July, 1984

10 9 8 7 6 5 4 3 2 1

POCKET and colophon are registered trademarks
of Simon & Schuster, Inc.

WOMAN'S DAY is a trademark of CBS, Inc.

Printed in the U.S.A.

To Dearest Pamela
A BEAUTIFUL WOMAN OF INFINITE GRACE;
AN INSPIRATION ALWAYS

Contents

Woman's Day®

Complete Guide to Entertaining

Introduction

To many people "entertaining" has a formidable ring to it. It can sound intimidating to someone who just wants to have a few friends in for dinner; but the simple desire to gather people together is the foundation of all good entertaining.

Perhaps the French term *recevoir* (to receive) more accurately describes what entertaining is all about. One does not merely bring people together, one provides for them as well. What and how one provides for them is what distinguishes a simple get-together from true entertaining.

A successful event, large or small, does not just happen; it is orchestrated. The several facets of that orchestration are detailed on the following pages, from selecting a date to correct table service, and even including the post-party cleanup.

Food, of course, has always been the centerpiece of entertaining, ever since Eve issued an invitation to share an apple. Courtships flourish, friends are made, contracts are signed, and honors are bestowed around the table. Life's milestones—birth, marriage, and death—are traditionally marked by "breaking bread" together.

Food, then, is a major part of this book. Appropriate recipes are included in chapters on Brunches and Luncheons, Tea Parties, Cocktail Parties and Buffets, Picnics and Barbeques, and Dinner Parties. Since dinner is the most popular form of entertaining, it gets the largest number of recipes.

Some people entertain with natural ease. They are the lucky ones. But anyone can entertain without anxiety, and every occasion can be a pleasure for both guests and host. Let's begin.

WHY ENTERTAIN?

Perhaps the question is better stated as "Why *not* entertain?" Just as holidays add gaiety and sparkle to the year, so do small private festivities. We are almost all social creatures who react positively to "togetherness." How often have you felt a little tired on the way to a party, only to find your spirits lifted once you were there? Entertaining and being entertained tend to refresh and enrich our lives. Without the break from routine, life would be pretty flat; entertaining provides the high notes.

No specific reason is necessary to give a party, though any number of occasions can be taken as an excuse for an event. A holiday is obvious, be it Christmas, New Year's, or the Fourth of July. Birthdays and anniversaries are other traditional dates. A new job or a promotion, a friend moving away, a colleague coming through town, welcoming a new couple on the block, even a bon voyage or welcome home to travelers are all causes for celebration. I once threw a "Cast-Off" party the night before a plaster cast was removed from my broken leg. Since I was handicapped in my movements and therefore limited in my cooking, nothing more than champagne and store-bought nibbles were served.

There is also business entertaining. This is often done at lunch. However, a dinner party is infinitely more convivial and usually more productive. Some people set a regular schedule for such parties, say every other Thursday, and somehow manage to stick to it. I find that it is better to try to make the evening seem as special and spontaneous as possible. No more than one or two business contacts should be invited at a time; the rest of the guests should be from other fields. If the entertaining is done in a restaurant, the host should make arrangements so that the bill is not presented at the table. If he is well known to the staff of the restaurant, a prior phone call can ensure that the check is held for his next visit; otherwise, he can slip away from the table and discreetly pay the check elsewhere. There is no point in emphasizing that it is a company evening by settling the bill in front of the guests.

Theater parties are also popular, but given the high cost of tickets these days, they too tend to be reserved for business entertaining. For more convivial results in large groups, try to get the same set of seats in two consecutive rows. This permits easy conversation at intermission time and eliminates the loud voices necessary when guests are strung out in a single row.

Once you've decided to have a party for whatever reason, pick the date carefully. Unless you are locked into a particular date by the nature of the event, check for conflicts. Is it a long weekend when many people will be out of town? Is there a large benefit show or an important football game scheduled for that day? If artists or art patrons are involved, for instance, confirm that no major opening is taking place at a museum or gallery that evening. This rule is less important for small parties where you know the interests of the guests, but with large affairs there is a risk that many people may already be committed to another function. Social calendars in local newspapers and magazines are helpful in checking out dates.

Now that you've decided to throw a party and have selected the date, next comes the most important part of your production—the cast of characters.

The Guest List and Invitations

Just as a good mix turns out a superior cocktail, a good mix of people makes a sparkling party. The smaller the party, the more important the guest list becomes, since each person carries more conversational weight; at large affairs people tend to chat for a few minutes, then move on.

Office parties belong right where the name indicates and not at your home on a Saturday night. If the entire guest list consists of office colleagues you are doing nothing but extending the work week. Begin with a nucleus of one or, at most, two couples from the office and add other friends from unrelated fields. Conversation is more interesting when input comes from different backgrounds.

I would also suggest that you avoid inviting only doctors, artists, schoolteachers, politicians, and so on, not only for conversational diversity, but to avoid any professional ego bruising. When you put a clutch of lawyers together you risk a remarkable and interminable display of one-upmanship.

If there is a guest of honor from out of town, give some thought to what sort of people he or she might like to meet. If he happens to be an expert on, say, Siamese fighting fish, he would certainly be interested in talking to other tropical fish fanciers. Ask the guest of honor if he has acquaintances in town whom he'd like you to invite. I have also found that an out-of-towner appreciates a list of the names of the other guests along with a few words about their professions. He can then join conversations more readily.

Time was when a hostess would just as soon call off a dinner party if the numbers of men and women weren't exactly even. I abandoned that archaic rule ages ago. There were occasions when the table was even but I decided that Mary would be a great asset to the evening and added her with no thought of pairing her with a man. Matchmaking is not necessarily part of being a good host or hostess. However, if a single woman is coming and lives close to other guests, it is thoughtful to suggest that they pick her up.

You can be a very misleading pronoun when inviting someone who has a steady friend, especially a live-in. Since *you* can be either singular or plural, careful phrasing is essential if you mean only the person to whom you are talking. You might say something like, "Just the other day Jim was saying that we haven't seen Alice in ages, so we were wondering if you could come for brunch next Sunday." That *you* refers strictly to Alice, and if she still shows up with Bumble Bob, you need less obtuse friends. On the other hand, if you want Alice to bring a friend, say so. On a written invitation, "and Escort" can be added after her name. She should then let you know if she is coming with someone and tell you his name and address. A personal invitation to him follows as a reminder.

Age groups should also be kept in mind to a minor degree. This is less important today since older people now tend to look and dress years younger than their chronological age, while younger people are more sophisticated for their years. Still, the hostess needs to be sensitive to certain parameters and generally should not include a 15-year-old son and his pal in a group of largely retired people.

Deciding on the number of people you can invite is simple if you're giving a sit-down dinner or buffet: you know precisely how many can comfortably sit at your table. For a barbecue, experience will show how many steaks or kebabs will fit on the grill. The real problem arises when you're planning a large reception, such as a cocktail party, wedding, or benefit. Just as airlines overbook, you are allowed to over-invite; in both cases, the critical question is, by how much? The rule of thumb used by caterers is that one-quarter to one-third of those invited will decline. So if you plan a cocktail party for 50, invite 65 to 70. For truly important occasions—a wedding, a surprise fortieth birthday party, a fiftieth wedding anniversary—the rate of attrition is much lower since every invitee will make a special effort to attend. Here you may lose no more than 15 percent, so, again using 50 as a base, invite 58 to 60. Inevitably, even beyond the original regrets, there will be a few last-minute cancellations. One cardinal rule: never plan an outdoor party so large that all the people cannot fit into the house. If you do, it will rain. Count on it.

Some hosts and hostesses try to handle large numbers of guests by the dubious practice of a double invitation list. For example, 25 people are invited for cocktails between 5 and 7, and another 25 between 6 and 8. The reasoning is that the ebb and flow of the crowd will always result in a manageable number. Invariably guests discover the ploy and begin to wonder which is the "in" list. Good friends who might have come together find themselves in opposite slots. Far better to restrict the guest list and plan two parties.

Invitations

Invitations should be mailed or phoned three to four weeks in advance for large affairs and about two weeks ahead for smaller parties. Though written invitations for small parties convey the impression of special attention, most people find the telephone the most expeditious way to issue invitations today. An immediate or prompt answer is guaranteed, giving you extra time to invite someone else in case of a refusal. You should give as much information as possible about the party: date, time, special reason or guest of honor, and dress. Give some idea of how large or small a party it will be. Guests tend to arrive later than specified at large receptions and to be more punctual for small affairs.

It is most important to give guests a true idea of the sort of dress code you want. It is of no help to them to say "come as you like," when you really want the men in jackets and the women in dresses instead of jeans. And tell all of them the same thing. Nothing makes a guest feel more uncomfortable than being over- or underdressed and it is unfair to put him or her in that position.

"Casual" and "informal" are often, mistakenly, used interchangeably. You can't be sure how the message is received at the other end of the phone, so be as specific as possible. In most large cities "informal" means dressing nicely but not black tie; "casual" should be used to indicate sports clothes. If asked, you can describe the sort of clothes you will wear. If you are inviting for a poolside party, of course, there is no problem.

One should also be specific about the sort of affair it will be. This is especially true if the time is not the usual hour for a party in your area. An invitation for 8:30 in New York City could easily be for dinner, but in Fosterville it might mean dessert and coffee. If there will be swimming, tennis, cards, dancing, movies—say so.

Depending on the custom in your city, a reminder card can be sent to follow up on a telephone conversation. I think it is advisable to do so. Informals are generally used, listing the guest's name and the date and time of the party. Dress (informal, black tie, white tie, costume, sports clothes, et cetera) goes in the lower right-hand corner, and "to remind" or *"pour memoire"* in the lower left-hand corner. Informals are also used for invitations without a prior telephone call; then R.S.V.P. is written in the lower left-hand corner instead of "to remind." Often people are difficult to reach by phone; in this case the written invitation is the most practical.

For large parties, especially those with themes, special invitations can be found at stationery or party stores. Bright and colorful cards help set the tone for a spirited affair. Inexpensive printing and color xeroxing open up the possibility for creating all sorts of fanciful invitations.

For formal functions, heavy white or cream-colored board cards are used, either entirely engraved, or partially engraved and filled in with specific information. Calligraphy is an especially handsome touch on invitations and envelopes for the most formal occasions. Calligraphers generally charge by the piece; keep in mind that they need plenty of time. While you're at it, have the calligrapher do the place cards, too.

Even in these days of fading sexism the wife generally handles the inviting and accepting of invitations, even if she does not know the business associates who are being invited. She should write or telephone the associate's wife. For a casual affair, the husband could conveniently extend the invitation during a conversation with his colleague, in which case his wife should follow up with a reminder card.

A common practice for large parties is to ask for "Regrets

Only." I tend to consider these second-class invitations, since they signal a huge affair and the fact that my presence really doesn't matter all that much. This form is practical for embassy receptions and other truly gigantic affairs where 300 or 400 people are invited; but for any private function I strongly urge asking for replies. One can never be certain how many people will actually show up when they have not had to make a real commitment. You could prepare for 75 celebrants and end up with 30.

In the unhappy event that a party must be canceled or postponed, it is always preferable to write a note, though the telephone can be used if time is short. In either case no explanation is required. It suffices to say something like, "We are very sorry, but we are going to have to cancel (or postpone) Friday's dinner." If you feel comfortable divulging the reason for the change, by all means cite it. If the party is postponed, indicate the new date if at all possible. However, if the new date is fixed at a later time, the hostess is still obliged to reinvite the same guests.

Good Guests

The fact that guests also have duties is often overlooked. The very first one is to reply promptly. If you must check with your spouse for a possible conflict, get back to your hostess as soon as possible. If for some reason you are unable to commit yourself until a later date, tell your hostess and leave it up to her to decide if she wants to wait to hear from you. Many times the table is small and she may want to fill it right away, rather than risk calling someone at the last minute and being turned down. And of course, once an invitation is accepted, only some urgent circumstance or illness is a legitimate excuse for bowing out. A later and more enticing invitation must, regretfully, be declined. Better offers just don't count when it comes to good manners.

Unless specific dress has been indicated, it is always flattering to your hosts to dress up; the fact that you have taken the care to arrive looking your best indicates to them that you consider their invitation something special. If you are unsure about how to dress, don't hesitate to call and ask. Nothing will spoil the evening for you faster than being overdressed or not dressed up enough.

Punctuality is important. For a luncheon or dinner, arriving five to ten minutes after the appointed hour is acceptable; fifteen minutes is the absolute limit. Embassy and official affairs require on-the-dot punctuality, even if it means you must arrive a few minutes early. But by no means should a guest arrive at a private home early. Those last minutes are precious to the hosts, as there are always more last-minute chores to do than one counted on. We sometimes sit in the car or walk around the block in order to arrive five minutes late. No one will blame you for being on the doorstep smack on time, but giving your hosts a few minutes of breathing time will be much appreciated.

To bring a gift, or not to bring a gift? Nothing is required, except for birthday parties and such, but it is a nice gesture as long as the gift is a small token. It should not be lavish enough to be construed as some sort of payment for the hospitality. If you know of some special interests of your hosts, an offering in that vein would be perfect. My husband often receives special bottles of wine, while friends bring me unusual or homemade foods. Chocolates are always appropriate, as are books and small plants. I happen to hate having cut flowers brought to me no matter how beautiful. If they are sent ahead, fine, but I do not want to spend time hunting for an appropriate vase and arranging the flowers when I should be chatting with guests. If they come in some small inexpensive jar or pot, I accept them with the greatest pleasure.

Newly arrived guests must be introduced by the hosts. If the group is small, say six to eight, it is best to present them to the gathering all at once. In larger groups, take the new arrivals to a small group, introduce them, and drop a few words about them to get the conversation going—"Fred and Suzy just returned from France where they cruised down the canals," or that sort of thing. And remember the old rule still stands: gentlemen are presented to ladies—"Fran, I would like you to meet Bob."

Now it is up to the guests to keep the conversation going. As a guest I feel an obligation to help the party work. The hostess did not invite me just because of my big brown eyes, but because she also felt that I would be compatible with the group. The guest who sits back and does not participate is rarely invited again. That is not to say that any single guest should try to be the "star" of the evening; just be lively and interested and have a good time.

It seems like a contradiction, but Americans have never been more interested in good and adventurous dining, and, at the same time, they have never been more diet-conscious. If you have been invited for a meal, you can be certain that the cook made a real effort to present special foods; his or her dining table is no place to diet. It is not necessary to overeat to show how much you've enjoyed the gratinéed scallops, but don't sit there and pick at your food and complain about calories. One meal isn't going to break your calorie campaign; enjoy tonight and cut down tomorrow.

If there are no ashtrays on the table, it tells you that you are not supposed to smoke at the table. Restrain yourself until after dinner when people who are bothered by smoke can back away.

When there is a guest of honor, he or she should leave first; otherwise, guests should begin drifting away at a reasonable hour, particularly on a week night. Don't linger in the doorway letting a chilly draft in or the air conditioning out, but sincerely and enthusiastically thank your hosts and be gone. Within the next day or so, either call or write a thank-you note mentioning some special food, person, conversation, or decoration that you especially admired. By citing some specific detail of the evening you make it clear that you were paying attention.

Party-Planning Strategy

Planning is without a doubt the hallmark of the person who entertains well. Advance planning helps you avoid unnecessary pitfalls. The two most important props needed for party planning are pencil and paper. Every special thing that should be done must be written down. The nervous or inexperienced hostess will find the written list welcome reassurance that she is not forgetting anything, and even the experienced or super-busy hostess who is juggling many things at once will find that the chart relieves her of remembering all the little details—a quick look, and nothing is left to chance.

It is best to make two worksheets—one an overall rundown on all specific preparations, and the second a shopping and cooking list. (These will be described in detail later on.) Once the basic kind of party is decided on (lunch, dinner, cocktails, buffet, picnic, tea), the three remaining questions are: large or small, formal or informal, and with or without help.

The patterns of entertaining have changed because people today often have less living space, but no matter how small your quarters, guests must be comfortable or it is unfair to invite them. This may mean having smaller, more frequent parties or using alternative spaces. You could borrow a friend's garage for a cocktail party or dance: festoon it with ribbons and balloons and turn it into a party palace. Use a public park for a picnic or, more innovatively, for a Sunday breakfast or brunch. Check cookout facilities at a local beach and plan a beach party complete with barbecue. In some cities there are cruise boats for rent, or regular or double-decker buses, streetcars, even sleighs in winter. Boxed suppers, complete with small wine flasks, provide easily portable refreshments.

For a party at home, take a good hard look around and try to figure out how to make the best use of your space. First, remove all knickknacks and clutter—the room will immediately appear larger. Put chairs and sofas against the walls in an L or U shape, leaving the center of the room clear for easy mobility. Keep the lighting dim in the center of the room and highlight the perimeter with spotlights, thus drawing the eye outward. Wherever possible use glass vases, bowls, and ashtrays to provide sparkle and a transparency that does not stop the eye. Use candles to identify the part of the room currently being used; for example, burn candles in the living room during the cocktail hour. When moving to another side of the same room or to an adjoining space, light candles in the new area and blow them out in the living room. Study any extra rooms and decide whether you can convert them into entertaining space with minimal effort. Card tables can be set up in the study, the kitchen, even the bedroom. Decide what you want to do, do it, and don't apologize because it is not Versailles.

The second question—the degree of formality—requires a bit more thought than simply deciding whether or not black tie will be the dress for the occasion. As discussed earlier, the degree of informality is equally important. Informal can mean suits and ties for the men and dresses for women, or it can mean casual wear—sports shirts and no ties for men and slacks, or even jeans, for women. Again, this information should be conveyed when the invitations are issued.

The last decision—help or no help—is usually resolved by the question of money. Today, hiring just one waiter to serve at a dinner party can cost far more than the food, and if you are pleased with his services and would like to have him back, it is wise to add a tip. Many people, therefore, choose to do without help for most small affairs. Naturally, the scope of the party also dictates whether help is necessary. It would be rather ostentatious to engage someone for a simple poolside party for a few friends, but if the same party is expanded to, say, 20 people and cloth-covered tables and chairs are provided, then a helping hand is quite in order. Help is mandatory when formal attire is worn.

Now is the time to start writing out your lists. If you are doing this for the first time, write down every single thing that must be done. At subsequent parties you will find that many of the procedures are repeated, so that one good party chart, with small variations, can be used over and over. No one entertains every day, or even every week, so many of the essential steps of party planning can be forgotten in surprisingly little time. If during the course of the preparations you find that something should be added or deleted, make a notation on the chart for future reference. The following chart is just a guide for the sort of chores that should be listed; your own plan may be very different. Be sure to factor some flexibility into the schedule for the small emergencies that always occur.

24

Three to Four Weeks Before:
 Decide on style of party and theme, if any.
 For very large party, rent extra equipment from a caterer, plan table decor and floral arrangements, shop for any party favors, plan menu.
 Make guest list.
 Write invitations or make phone calls.
 Hire extra help, if necessary.

Two Weeks Before:
 Plan menu and make shopping and cooking schedule. (See Menu-Planning, pages 37–41.)
 Send reminder notes to those you called.
 For single parents or apartment dwellers in small quarters, call friends and make overnight arrangements for the children.
 If children are old enough, include a movie in the evening as a special treat.

One Week Before:
 Plot rearranging of furniture, if necessary.
 Plan table decor and floral arrangements.
 Order flowers.
 Check candle supply.
 Check that table linens are fresh.
 Check bar supplies—liquor, wine, mixers, soft drinks.
 Shop for canned goods and other staples.

Four Days Before:
 Write out menu cards and place cards.
 Polish silver.

Three Days Before:
 Clean house.

Two Days Before:
 Start making extra ice and store in plastic bags.
 Do the bulk of the shopping, leaving most perishable items for later.

Start cooking those dishes to be served cold and those that
reheat well.

Type out menu and final food preparation tasks for serving
help, if using.

One Day Before:

Buy rest of fresh food.

Make seating plan.

Have hair done.

Select party clothes for yourself and spouse and check
that they are in good order.

Wash lettuce and other greens, dry well, and store in
plastic bags.

If extra tables are being used, arrange them now, provided
no small children will undo them.

Select records if playing background music.

Party Day:

(during the day)

Finish cooking.

Buy fresh bread.

Set out linen and one place setting as a pattern for serving
help, or set table.

Place candles in all rooms to be used for party.

Arrange flowers.

Put white wine in refrigerator.

Set out ashtrays and matches.

Give house a once-over.

Run dishwasher so it will be empty.

Check closet—enough room and hangers?

Clear living room of newspapers and magazines.

Set up bar.

Set out serving platters and silver.

Empty garbage.

(3 hours before)

If children are staying overnight with friends, drop them
off.

(2 hours before)
> If children are staying home, feed them early; get them to bed, or allow a quick hello to guests—and good-bye.
> Take time to relax! Fifteen minutes with your feet up will do wonders.
> Dress.

(1 hour before)
> Open red wine.
> Put finishing touches on meal.
> Stock bar with pitcher of water, ice, lemon zests and slices.
> Set out snacks in cocktail area.
> If pets are pesky or a guest is allergic to them, lock them up.

(15 minutes before)
> Light lamps and candles (not table candles).
> Pour yourself a drink.

Once the table is set, go through the menu course by course and put out all the china and cutlery needed. It is best to stack or arrange dishes and platters in the order in which they will be used, putting the last to be used (usually dessert) farthest away. If coffee and liqueurs are to be served in another room, put the glasses, cups, saucers, teaspoons, and sugar there, along with a trivet to hold the hot coffeepot.

A nicely laid table is not put together in five minutes; it requires more time than you think. Women who spend all day at the office should set the table the night before. If a cleaning lady comes in, have her do the table; lay out the table linen and one place setting yourself as a pattern.

Everyone finds his or her own style of entertaining and the most efficient way to handle a party alone. Some people have found rolling tea carts an invaluable aid: one shelf holds clean dishes and cutlery for subsequent courses, while the other shelf is left empty for dirty dishes removed from the table. The cart is usually placed next to the hostess. I read of one couple where both host and hostess were equipped with rolling carts, and everyone marveled at the expediency of the system. Frankly, it strikes me as too much of a factory-line production, with the flashing of silver and china at both ends of the table creating more show than grace.

Today the single man or woman who entertains often has a wider choice of entertaining schemes than couples. Telephone invitations, instead of written cards, are almost taken for granted. He or she can also easily eschew structured meals and invite friends and business colleagues for something as simple as viewing a popular or important television program while sharing a buffet supper. She or he can make a splash by taking everyone out to a simple restaurant (barbecue, crab house, pasta, deluxe hamburgers) and return home for dancing or dessert, or both. A fun evening can be based on inviting all the guests to come and help cook dinner.

At times, however, a more formal sit-down meal is appropriate, either because of the occasion or the guest list, or simply because you are a good cook. Doing it all yourself requires very careful menu planning. Serving the first course at the end of the cocktail hour before everyone comes to the table is an excellent device to reduce jumping up and down during the meal. Cold or hot soup is one efficient choice; others are cold pasta salads served on salad plates (be sure to cut the pasta into short lengths that can easily be managed with just a fork), shrimp and a dab of sauce held on artichoke petals artfully arranged on a round platter, a slice of cold rolled omelet soufflé which easily submits to a fork alone, or perhaps steak Tartare on strips of warm toast.

It is the most natural thing in the world for the single person to ask a friend to be host or hostess at the other end of the table and to see to it that wine and water glasses are filled. Just as women traditionally have been pegged as the cooks, men have been the self-appointed sommeliers. Today, however, many men are superb cooks and many women are extremely knowledgeable about wine. But if the single host lacks the latter expertise, he or she should use a reliable wine merchant or consult a friend.

Guests who want to help—now there's a thorny subject! My kitchen is well organized and I alone know where things should go. I don't allow it and have been known to snap at those who follow me into the kitchen and plunk down dirty plates precisely where I planned to arrange the next platter. I even dislike having my husband get up and help, but I can't hiss at him with guests in the house. If one person gets up, then others feel obliged to follow suit and soon the whole party has been transferred to the kitchen. I feel everyone should sit still and keep the conversation going. Don't help me in my house and I won't help you in yours—promise. Now, not everyone feels as strongly as I do on the matter, so if you feel your host or hostess might appreciate a little help, offer, but don't insist if your offer is refused.

As dishes are cleared, scrape them quickly and stack them out of the way or place them in the dishwasher. An empty dishwasher is critical for speed here. One can accomplish this operation most discreetly if the chatter at the table continues, making your short absence less noticeable—another reason to discourage guests from helping out. But please don't run the disposal while people are at the table. The sound of the food they didn't eat being ground to bits and washed away ruins the pleasure of dining and reduces eating to simple physical activity.

For the smoothest running of dinner parties, menu-planning is the critical factor. It's discussed more fully in the chapter devoted to the subject, pages 37–41. No more than three courses should be served. I have often served vegetables separately following the main course, but on the same plate. Select a first course that can be put in place before guests are called to the table, either a cold dish or something super-hot that will cool to a manageable temperature by the time everyone's seated. A cold main course is also a clever way to avoid last-minute fussing in the kitchen. Starting with a hot soufflé is risky business. Once baked it must be served immediately, and you can count on at least one very late guest on this occasion. Dessert soufflés, however, are quite manageable since guests are generally happy to wait for them.

A guest can be asked to help pour wine at one end of the table while the host pours at the other end. Have the wine at the table before sitting down.

Help and Equipment

If you have decided to engage help, the next question is how much? One waiter or waitress can comfortably handle 8 to 10 guests at an informal seated dinner or 12 to 16 at a buffet. At formal dinners count on a minimum of one waiter for each 6 to 8 guests. A barman for every 25 guests at a cocktail party works out nicely.

The table setting, stocking the bar, last-minute preparations, and the making of hors d'oeuvres usually can all be left for the waiter. Of course, the more you leave for him to do, the earlier he must arrive, which means extra charges. The most cost-efficient help to employ is someone who can cook well enough not to ruin what you've prepared, can serve nicely, and leaves an impeccable kitchen.

The best way to find good help is through references; keep a file of the names and phone numbers of waiters and waitresses you've observed at friends' homes. Remember, money alone doesn't guarantee competent help. Local caterers often have large rosters of part-time staffers and can supply you with a waiter. Generally, you pay no fee for this service; the caterer bills you and takes his percentage from the money paid the waiter.

Many college personnel offices have names of students anxious to earn some extra money. Usually these young people are very pleasant, bright, efficient, and helpful. They can serve at the table if given proper instructions (white shirts or blouses are sufficient uniform), do an excellent job of bartending, and handle valet parking for large weddings or a formal ball. Bartending and cooking schools are other sources to tap, and don't forget neighbors' teenagers or even your own. If you don't need them to help with serving, consider just having them clean up the kitchen. Whatever their services, they should be paid some fee.

If you are having a large open-house party and have hired someone to staff the checkroom, please make it quite clear that absolutely no tipping is allowed. At times checkroom staff will put out a discreet little dish with some money in it to encourage contributions. This is fine for a hotel or restaurant, but offensive in a private home.

Serving personnel should be wearing impeccably clean clothes. For lunch, white jackets are more appropriate than black tie for waiters. Waitresses have more of a selection—a white or light-colored uniform or a black one with white apron and trim for lunch, and only the latter for dinner.

Rental Equipment

If you rarely throw a large party, it makes sense to rent the necessary supplies. However, if you find that you invite large crowds more than twice a year, it becomes worthwhile to invest in inexpensive supplies, providing you have room to store them. Here is a short list of items you might need to rent on a one-time basis:

coat rack and hangers	large coffee urns
extra chairs, straight-legged or folding	glasses
bridge tables	dishes, cups, saucers
extra-large round tables	silverware
tablecloths and napkins	wine buckets
large platters	candelabra
	tents or marquees

The classified section of the local newspaper or the yellow pages of the telephone directory are excellent sources for special needs. Here is a sampling of some listings to keep in mind when planning parties:

Amusement Devices	Caterers
Automobile Rental	Chauffeur Services
Awnings and Canopies	Chinaware and Glassware Rental
Ballrooms	
Bartending Services	Dance Floors, Portable (caterers can often help here, too)
Boat Rental	
Calligraphers	

Dance Instruction
Decoration (or Party)
    Contractors
Entertainers
Favors and Souvenirs
Flags and Banners
Florists (also for plant rental)
Formal Wear—Rental
Furniture Rental
Games and Game Supplies
Limousine Services
Motion Picture Equipment
    and Supplies—Rental
Orchestras and Bands

Party-Planning Services
Party Supplies
Photographers
Sound Systems and
    Equipment
Stationers
Table Decoration—Rental
Television Rental (especially
    useful for such events as
    election-night parties)
Theatrical Agencies (for
    performers—mimes,
    magicians, clowns,
    comedians)

Table Linens and Decorations

Just as styles of entertaining have changed, so have table settings. No longer do cupboards bulge with 102-piece china sets. Finger bowls are rarely seen except at official functions. Heavily embroidered tablecloths are disappearing as fast as hand laundries. Indeed, table decorating today is an art form that thrives on imagination and flair. The predictability of earlier table settings is gone forever.

One might ask if it matters to lavish that much time and care on how the table looks. Of course it does! This is the setting— the frame, if you will—for several hours of conviviality. Although an attractive table won't mask a burned roast, it certainly will enhance what is put upon it. Every meal, even a family meal, is a small celebration of sorts, and as such should be dressed for the role. We meet at the table three times a day, far too often to put up with a dull or unattractive display. Treat yourselves as well as you treat company.

Attractive should not be confused with expensive. Plain white pottery plates can look as impressive as the finest china when placed on a colorful cloth. Three or four irises and some broad green leaves from the garden can be just as effective as a florist's $40 bouquet. Choose mildly scented flowers so that their aroma will not conflict with that of the food. Pretty as they are, freesias won't do, nor will geraniums, marigolds, eucalyptus leaves, boxwood stems, or gardenias.

The best way to create striking table settings is to build a wardrobe of linens, then mix and match them to strike the mood you want to achieve. Tablecloths and napkins do not have to match; in fact, napkins in contrasting colors can act as accent notes on the table. One clever scheme for covering round tables is to use a solid-color floor-length undercloth and top it with a patterned square cloth slightly larger than the tabletop. This arrangement is as practical as it is pretty, since often only the smaller top piece needs to be laundered.

Go beyond the table linen departments and search out attractive alternatives such as batik cloth, brightly patterned Scandinavian cotton drapery material, linen dish toweling by the yard, bed sheets, and cotton dress fabric. Don't be afraid of black-and-white patterns (preferably geometric); they look cool and dramatic. Use white napkins against the black-and-white, or switch to a color, like red, for an extra fillip. Place mats can be made of the same fabrics. If the table is a handsome wood, occasionally leave it bare, but take care that the plates are not so hot that they will leave marks.

Place mats and runners are particularly efficient when storage space is limited as both fit neatly into drawers. To help preserve their fresh look, slip pieces of stiff cardboard cut to place-mat size to separate every 10 or so mats. The cardboard supports allow you to reach the lower part of the stack without wrinkling the mats on top.

Creased cloths are less of a problem with today's almost magically wrinkle-free fabrics. Usually, I find, they do need just the slightest bit of touching up with the iron, but they really do remain fresh-looking during storage. If a crease or two does develop, smoothing it firmly with the palm of the hand usually suffices to put the cloth back into spanking-fresh order. Straw place mats, of course, are completely trouble free. Look for some of the unusual examples coming from China; they are good-looking and inexpensive.

I am a collector of dishes, not only antiques but also attractive, well-designed contemporary pottery and china. I find it rather dull to look at the same pattern from soup to chocolate mousse. You will be pleasantly surprised at what handsome dishes are available when you don't insist on a complete set.

Glassware, too, can be of different patterns, preferably not etched. People seriously interested in wine dislike distortion when studying the color and clarity of the heady liquid.

The possibilities for centerpieces are almost limitless. Beyond flowers, consider the impact of tureens, attractive bottles, shallow trays, baskets, low bowls and vases, fruits and vegetables, dried flowers, ceramic figures, small sculptures, seashells, mineral rocks, silver boxes, craggy driftwood, paperweights, or colored glass balls in a glass bowl. A single dahlia bloom submerged in water in a glass bowl is pure drama. If objects are small, mass them together for scale.

There are some rules to keep in mind when planning the table decoration. The centerpiece should be low enough not to interfere with across-the-table vision. Don't use any object on the table, no matter how pretty, if it is unstable. Knees do bump tables. Candles are best when they're very short, such as votive lights, or quite tall. Flickering candlelight near eye level is annoying and uncomfortable. And no scented candles please; the aroma will conflict with that of the food.

It goes without saying that the napery should be spotless, the glasses sparkling, and the silver gleaming. The pristine look of the table is enhanced by a smooth cloth. Do not crowd folded cloths together in storage, lest the creases become sharp. Long rollers from drapery fabric shops make ideal storage vehicles for smaller cloths; wrap ironed cloths around the rollers and they will remain smooth and creaseless.

Lighting is another consideration. The ideal ambience is created by somewhat dim lighting overall highlighted by candles at the table and throughout the room.

Party Themes

At times the decorating of both the table and house will be dictated by the occasion, such as a wedding, Christmas, or

New Year's Eve, but one can also create a party around a theme. The following list suggests some themes that make for good parties:

- Hawaiian Luau—The hallmark of this outdoor party is the lavish array of exotic island food. *Hawaiian Cookbook* by Roana and Gene Schindler (Dover Books) is an excellent source for authentic recipes.
- April Fool's Day—Full of tricks, of course.
- July 4th
- July 14th—France's Bastille Day, the equivalent of our July 4; make it a red-white-and-blue party, but with Gallic flair.
- Halloween
- Treasure Hunt—Hide small gifts around the house, garden, or both.
- Classic Movie Night—Rent a movie from a film or video library and show it after an early dinner; dessert and coffee can be served while the reels are being changed or after the film is over.
- Mother's Day and Father's Day
- Games Night—Send invitations with a choice of games to be selected when guests reply. Some easy-to-handle games are poker, roulette, Monopoly, bingo, checkers, Scrabble, and backgammon. Set the games in various rooms, even in the kitchen, and award prizes to the winners. Serve a buffet midway through the evening.
- Teenage Disco Party
- Diet Lunch for Ladies—Many good diet cookbooks are now on the market. Look especially for the *Better Homes and Gardens Dieter's Cookbook,* Barbara Gibbons's *Slim Gourmet* series, and Jean Nidetch's *Weight Watchers* books.
- Valentine's Day
- Spanish Cocktail Party—The Spanish are late-night people and this habit is reflected in their cocktail parties which usually begin no earlier than 9 P.M. The abundant finger food is served in courses; this is a full meal eaten in small bits. Here is an adaptation of the traditional fare: fish (steamed mussels served cold with sauce, homemade deep-fried codfish balls, hot or cold shrimp, scallops ceviche); meats (meat-

balls, marinated boiled beef cubes, thin slices of chicken breast rolled around asparagus tips or strips of roasted red pepper, hot minature lamb kebabs); vegetables (deep-fried mushrooms, marinated cauliflower florets, broiled mushroom caps stuffed with duxelles, broiled kebabs combining cubed eggplant with feta cheese and cherry tomato); dessert (petits fours, miniature cream puffs and eclairs, brownies, strawberries with powdered sugar, chocolates, mints); Irish coffee.

- Christmas Caroling
- New Year's Day Open House
- Formal English Tea—Cucumber and cress sandwiches are obligatory.
- Smorgasbord—Two good sources for inspiration and recipes are *Favorite Swedish Recipes,* edited by Selma Wifstrand (Dover Publications) and *Snacks and Sandwiches* from The Good Cook series (Time-Life Books). Both volumes are illustrated, but the smorgasbord spread in *Snacks and Sandwiches* is especially descriptive and easy to follow.
- Barn Dance—It's even fun in a garage.
- Zodiac Party
- Covered-Dish Party—Each guest brings an unspecified dish.
- Prose or Poetry Readings—Put together a group that meets regularly in different homes at cocktail time or after dinner for dessert and coffee during orations.
- After-Theater Supper
- Post-Football-Game Supper
- Supper after Christmas Midnight Mass
- Kitchen Party—This, of course, depends on the size of the kitchen. Informal suppers after the theater or sports events can be served and eaten in the kitchen. To handle larger crowds, use the kitchen as a buffet and provide enough table space in other rooms or supply trays that can rest on the lap. By using the kitchen for buffet service, space elsewhere can be kept clear for dancing.
- Children's Cooking Party—This makes a wonderful birthday party. Either have the group cook the birthday meal (pizza, hamburgers, or the like), just the cake, or batches of cookies.
- No-Hunt Breakfast—This means rather substantial fare:

Welsh rabbit, creamed chicken in patty shells, Smithfield ham, kippers, hot biscuits.

- Waffle Gala—Provide stacks of steaming-hot waffles and an assortment of toppings: creamed chicken, creamed chipped beef, sautéed chicken livers, maple syrup, bacon, honey, and, naturally, lots of butter. The same hot waffles become dessert when topped with fresh fruit, chocolate syrup, jams, hot butterscotch, or simply powdered sugar and orange liqueur.
- Cooking Demonstration—If you have a dish you are particularly proud of, move the cocktail hour into the kitchen so guests can watch you prepare dinner. Or let a friend put on the show instead.
- Anniversary—When an anniversary is an important one it is easy to build a party around the time-honored gifts. Diamond, gold, and silver are easy, but iron may tax your ingenuity. According to the *World Almanac,* this is the traditional list with *a few allowable* revisions in parentheses.

1st—Paper	14th—Ivory
2nd—Cotton	15th—Crystal
3rd—Leather	20th—China
4th—Linen (Silk)	25th—Silver
5th—Wood	30th—Pearl
6th—Iron	35th—Coral (Jade)
7th—Wool (Copper)	40th—Ruby
8th—Bronze	45th—Sapphire
9th—Pottery (China)	50th—Gold
10th—Tin (Aluminum)	55th—Emerald
11th—Steel	60th—Diamond
12th—Silk	75th—Diamond
13th—Lace	

Menu Planning

Menu planning does not mean simply putting together some of the specialties of the house. It involves composing a well-balanced meal that also minimizes the pressures on the cook.

Be honest with yourself and don't overestimate or underestimate your culinary abilities. If you reach too high, you are only asking for additional and unnecessary pressures; it is far better to be conservative and successful than daring and sorry. On the other hand, there is no reason to undersell your skills. If you can bone a chicken and stuff it, by all mean do. Guests won't be intimidated; they'll love it. Whatever your level of culinary expertise, if there is any question about a recipe, first run it through the kitchen for the family, allowing enough lead time to practice it again if necessary.

Keep in mind that hospitality should not be confused with overfeeding your guests. I consider it a great compliment when friends say, "What a delicious meal, and I don't feel at all heavy." On the other hand, I would feel that something were wrong (Thanksgiving aside) if the comment were, "What a great meal; I can't move." This is not a plug for meager meals, just sensible ones.

If you really can't cook and don't care to, you can do something quite different with good prepared food. It is always better to present good ready-made food than to serve poorly done homemade dishes. You might offer a Sunday brunch consisting of a large variety of breads and buns accompanied by exceptional jams and cheeses. Or put out a good delicatessen spread of cold cuts and salads, plus a selection of beers and wines. A shellfish raw-bar party is another ploy. If you know of a *good* Chinese carryout shop or bakery, buy dim-sum to steam at home; on pretty plates they look very special. You might even try Beef Fondue, which requires no skill, since the guests cook their own meat.

You should begin plotting the meal by deciding on the one dish you most want to do. If it is rich, then the other courses should be light. For example, if the main course is standing beef rib roast and Yorkshire pudding, the meal should begin with something like a clear soup with julienned vegetables, a cold artichoke vinaigrette, or a salad of sliced mushrooms with blanched turnip strips and bean sprouts. Select either string beans or asparagus to accompany the beef. Finally, finish the meal with poached pears or peaches with raspberry sauce, or a coffee granita and cookies.

Now let's take the opposite case and say you have decided

that the main course will be poached chicken breasts with a light mushroom sauce accompanied by wild rice. To precede it a more substantial first course would be in order, perhaps a hot onion tart or a lobster bisque. Salad should follow the chicken, and the meal could finish with a pastry.

The gargantuan meals of Diamond Jim Brady's era are mercifully a thing of the past; quality, not quantity, is today's motto. People are paying more attention to food, not just from the standpoint of health, but also from that of gustatory pleasure. Preparing fewer dishes means that you can lavish more time on each of them.

If you are handling the cooking and serving all by yourself, it is almost mandatory to select dishes that tolerate advance preparation; you might even want to start cooking several evenings before the event, after work. Let's see how the first menu cited above stands up to this criterion. With one small exception—the mushrooms must be sliced just before being tossed with the other ingredients—all of the first course possibilities and the desserts can be prepared in advance. That leaves just the main course to attend to on the day of the event, and this can be managed easily since the meat bakes for several hours and needs almost no attention, except to have its internal temperature checked periodically to avoid overcooking. The Yorkshire pudding batter can be prepared before the cocktail hour and baked toward the end of the roasting period.

While doing the advance cooking, always keep in mind that anything that will be reheated must be slightly undercooked at first. It is always possible to simmer a little longer if something is underdone, but a limp string bean can never be brought back to life.

Color is also an important aspect of any well-planned menu. A dinner starting with marinated scallops followed by poached chicken breasts with mornay sauce and rice and ending with floating island might have guests wondering if the cook had been snow-blinded by a blizzard. All that white could be relieved by a few red or green lettuce leaves under the scallops, serving wild or brown rice with the chicken, and ending the meal with strawberry tartlets.

The menu should also contain an interesting combination of

textures. When a custardy tart opens the meal, make certain there is a very crisp element in the main course, perhaps carrot sticks briefly simmered in chicken stock.

I have found that a cold main course is a wonderful stratagem for easy entertaining, and not just in the summertime. Its principal advantage is that it can usually be prepared at least a day ahead, or even longer in the case of pâtés. With the most important part of the meal out of the way, the cook can be far more relaxed; there is no danger of overcooking or undercooking in a last-minute flurry of activity. Cold main dishes also permit you to consider a wider range of foods: the above-mentioned pâtés; meat, vegetables, or fish encased in aspic; poached meats with mayonnaise-based sauces (Italy's famed *Vitello Tonnato* is a superb example); meat and fish salads. Before a cold entree, the first course, naturally, must be hot. Sometimes a hot vegetable and cold dessert follow the main dish, but at other times I shift directly to a hot dessert. This unusual rhythm of food presentation commands much more attention from your guests. The formula has been so successful for me that I recently wrote a book of such menus, all with pâtés as the main course (*Pâté: The New Main Course for the '80s*).

Know your audience before you venture to serve anything that borders on the exotic or unusual. Some people have strong prejudices against things like tongue, tripe, sea urchins, sweetbreads, brains, or snails, delicious as they are. Another risky category is raw foods—sashimi and sushi, steak Tartare, and carpaccio. Not everyone likes oysters, raw or cooked.

No one who entertains and is interested in fine cooking should be without a thorough general cookbook, such as *The Joy of Cooking* or *The Fannie Farmer Cookbook*. They are invaluable for the great amount of technical information packed into the volumes, and none of it in mysterious scientific terms. By helping you understand what is happening to the food on the stove or in the oven, they are teaching you to cook, not just to reproduce recipes. Though these books concentrate on American cooking, they encompass many other cuisines.

Once you've mastered the basics, you're ready to branch out to other cuisines and specialties. *Mastering the Art of*

French Cooking is a brilliant package of French classics. Look to Marcella Hazan and Giuliano Bugialli for Italian inspiration. No matter what cuisine you choose to explore, there is a good book out there to show the way.

Food magazines, women's magazines, and the food sections of newspapers provide a steady stream of innovative ideas for menus, new recipes, and table decorations.

Shopping and Cooking Lists

Once the menu has been drawn up, it is time to make the shopping and cooking lists. Read over each recipe and check your supplies to find out what you're missing. Make one list for an advance shopping trip to gather staples and fresh produce for those dishes that will be cooked in advance. I have devised a scheme for the second list that combines the cooking schedule and the remaining shopping. Let us say dinner is scheduled for Friday. I make up a chart for Wednesday, Thursday, and Friday. In the Wednesday block I write down what dishes can be cooked that far in advance: frozen desserts, soups, toasted almonds, pastry crust. In the same block I write in red* what fresh foods must be purchased for cooking Wednesday and Thursday. Thursday is similarly inscribed—one could prepare cold custard desserts, poached fruits, fruit sauces, dessert sauces, cakes, stewed or braised meats, salad dressing. Thursday's red notes might be fish, lettuce, watercress, and other perishables that will be used on Friday. Friday's work schedule will finish the recipe list (it's surprisingly small by now), including things like coffee, washing lettuce for salad, making hollandaise, and any meats or fish that are being cooked from scratch. The items listed in red are rarely more than bread and flowers.

One of the great pleasures in working with such a chart is being able to see all the lines drawn through the items as they are completed. It gives me a great sense of accomplishment, and I suspect it will do the same thing for you.

---

* In the sample schedule and list that follows, those items that I would write in red ink appear in italics.

Work Plan

Aug. 15—
Plan welcome-home dinner for Fosters, back from China.
Anyone special they want? Date: Thursday, Sept. 16,
7:30

Guest list: 8, plus Fosters
Make calls

Aug. 25–28—
Send reminders

Menu:
Mussel Cocktail
Hot Pork Roll with Mustard Sauce
Gingered Carrots
Apricot-Orange Cream
Call liquor store; which Calif. dry Chenin Blanc, Chablis,
Zin Rosé? Asti Spumante for dessert? Deliver Sept. 9

Sept. 4 –8 —
Need extra leaf for table
Red cloth, alternate pink & blue napkins (arranged in wine
glass)
Buy pink & blue candles
Buy fans in Chinatown for centerpiece (fans and flowers in
straw bread basket flanked with candles)
Add bourbon & sherry to wine delivery
Make hair appointment for 15th

Sept. 10–12—
Write menu & place cards
Polish silver

Sept. 13—
    Clean house

Sept. 15—
    Seating plan
    Beauty salon—2:30
    Choose and check clothes

Sept. 16, day—
    Touch up house
    Set table
    Chill wine
    Ashtrays in den and living room
    Closet OK?
    Check bar
    Put out platters & silver
    Candles in hallway
    Reheat lamb stew for children

6:30 —
    Set up bar & ice
    Pots & pans for pork & carrots
    Dress

7:15—
    Light candles in hallway

Check Staples

olive oil   white bread
dry vermouth/orange liqueur   sugar
garlic   cornstarch
butter   vinegar

celery salt
thyme
nutmeg
allspice

sage
oregano
bay leaf
dry mustard

Shopping List—Mon. or Tues.

3 lemons
2 pounds carrots
piece fresh ginger
3 seedless oranges
½ pound dried apricots
1 pint heavy cream
½ dozen eggs

Cooking and Shopping Plan

Tuesday
Mustard sauce
Apricot-Orange Cream
Mayonnaise

Wednesday
Steam mussels and marinate
Pork Roll
Gingered Carrots

3 pints mussels
2 pounds pork shoulder
½ pound ham
Sour cream
Parsley
Lettuce

Thursday
Mussel sauce
Reheat Pork Roll
Finish carrot sauce

Fresh bread
Flowers

The Indispensable Log

If the reader is getting the idea that paper and pencil are as important in planning parties as cooking and decorating talents, he is right. Every line that is written down is another step toward a smooth operation. Even after the party there is more writing to do—make a record of the event for future reference.

Use any sort of notebook. My party log is a loose-leaf folder. First write the date, time, guest list, and, for seated meals, the seating plan. Add a few descriptive words about the table linen and decoration, then record the menu and wines. You will find it very helpful to note how much food was prepared—for example, one recipe or double the recipe. Then add a note to indicate whether the amount was just right, too little, or too much. This is an important gauge when planning the next party at which similar food is served. Jot down the names of help brought in and how they worked out. Also critique the evening—what worked well, what went wrong, what would you change.

In the back of my log I have an additional record: a list of frequent guests in alphabetical order (I leave several spaces between names for later additions). After the names I jot down the dates they were here. If you do a lot of entertaining, a quick check will help prevent having the same people together too often. You can either flip back to the party record and see if the Ascots and the Palmers were invited at the same time, or simply scan the dates beside the names. Not that the Ascots and the Palmers should never meet again under your roof, but perhaps they would also enjoy meeting other of your friends.

Another very practical use for this guest list is to record friends' allergies. We have one friend who is allergic to red wine, fish, and mustard. Who's likely to remember all that? Jot down reactions to animals also (it may mean locking up the pets) and to flowers or plants.

The writing of the various lists and charts will not take very long; it actually takes far longer to explain it than to do it. But at every subsequent party you will be grateful for the information they hold. The party worksheet combined with the record log will be invaluable guidelines. No professional party planner could survive without lists and charts. Give yourself that same support system.

Tips for Before, During, and After the Party

• Keep calm, keep calm, keep calm. It cannot be said too often. A nervous host or hostess will have more mishaps than a composed one and will also give guests the jitters.

• Plan little rest periods for yourself during preparations.

• Even though people are cutting back on smoking these days, make sure there are plenty of ashtrays out in the reception area. Have extra ashtrays in reserve to exchange for used ones so that the odor doesn't become heavy and offensive.

• Make sure there's an umbrella stand near the front door.

• Have some sort of table or flat surface near the front door where women can put their handbags while they remove their coats.

• Guest books are seldom used these days, except in diplomatic circles or when entertaining expenses are deducted from taxes. But having a book for guests to sign makes a wonderful souvenir for the guest of honor on special occasions such as a wedding, anniversary, christening, bridal or baby shower, farewell party, housewarming, or graduation party. Handsome leather volumes can be bought from stationers and embossed with the name of the guest of honor and the date. But the book need not be that expensive; any handsome notebook would do, especially if imaginatively covered with photographs, wrapping paper, or fabric.

• The distribution of party favors is another custom of the past that should sometimes be revived. Favors never fail to give a party a lift. They need not be lavish: a pretty flower for each woman, a Christmas-tree bauble at holiday time, a small can of black-eyed peas at a New Year's Eve party, a small bundle of fresh herbs from your garden, a tiny basket of chocolates, or a fan at a summer or prom party. I am especially fond of placing beribboned nosegays on the dessert plates of the women; the gentlemen always end up with buttonières offered by the ladies.

• For a nighttime party around the pool, create a sparkling effect by setting candles afloat by anchoring votive lights on aluminum foil.

• For nighttime parties, place candles in old jars of any kind and tuck them in spots around the garden to create a fairyland look. In the dark who can tell the difference between a crystal hurricane lamp and a mayonnaise glass?

• Ice buckets will chill wine faster than the refrigerator. Put the bottle in first, add plenty of ice, and fill with water. Don't use the freezer, which can freeze the cork into place and make it very difficult to remove; this is especially true for champagne bottles.

• There can never be too many glasses or too much ice.

• Try to put flowers in every room, even if it's only one bloom; don't forget the bathroom.

• Use cotton flannel under tablecloths to give a softer look to the linen, protect the tabletop from heat or wine stains, and muffle the sound of china, glassware, and silver.

• Never apologize for food mishaps. If the leg of lamb is too well done, just ignore it; some people like it that way. If the soufflé isn't baked enough, casually mention that you prefer it with a lot of soft center as sauce. If the frozen soufflé didn't quite freeze, whip it, serve it in small bowls, and call it custard ice cream. By apologizing for a less-than-perfect dish you simply call attention to it and force everyone to vehemently disagree with you and claim they love it as it is.

• Keep extra forks handy to replace a dropped one without an embarrassing to-do.

• I no longer put ashtrays on the table, but you should always keep a small stack of ashtrays and matches near both ends of the table in case a guest pulls out a cigarette.

• Use attractive ceramic tiles as wine coasters.

• Expand round tables by using a folding poker table top.

• Have extra small tables and chairs available for small groupings at buffet parties.

• Serve warm food on warm plates. Five minutes in a 175-degree oven will bring them to the proper temperature. Do not overheat plates; they can burn guests' fingers, continue cooking any food put on them, and tend to emit a ceramic odor that interferes with the aroma of the food.

• As silverware is taken from the table, place it in a basin of hot soapy water. Wash and dry the pieces later, or drain off the soapy water and re-cover them with plain hot water for attention in the morning. Do not let silver drain dry after washing or it will be spotted.

• Wine glasses should be washed by hand or put through the dishwasher without detergent. A thin film and an odor cling to glasses washed in the usual way; this is referred to in the wine trade as "detergent stink." I use a detergentless cycle for all glasses, coffee saucers, soup bowl saucers, and any other dishes that need only a light washing. Lipstick stains will not always come off the glasses even with detergent and sometimes require separate washing.

• Remove sterling silver tops from salt shakers and replace them with corks cut to fit. Wash and dry the tops and store them separately. Salt corrodes silver and if the tops are left in place permanently, they will soon be pockmarked as the silver disappears around the holes.

• When stored, silver hollowware should be closely wrapped in silvercloth or airtight plastic wrap. Do not use rubber bands.

• Fill a basin with hot water and prewash solution and soak

the napkins overnight in it. They will be much easier to wash the next day.

• Red wine stains should be attended to immediately. Rub the stain with wet salt and let it stand at least six hours. Club soda also removes red wine spots because of the sodium it contains.

• If you have a red vinegar barrel, collect leftover red and white nonsparkling wines and add them to the barrel. If you insist on white wine vinegar only, then you are limited to leftover white wine.

Emergency Shelf

If good friends drop in and you'd like to ask them to stay for something to eat, you must be prepared. Here are some items to keep on hand that will make it possible to issue a spur-of-the-moment supper invitation and really mean it.

Pantry Shelf

crackers
nuts
pasta
rice
canned soups, especially red
    madrilene consommé
canned beef and chicken
    broth
barbecue sauce
tomato juice
cannellini beans
chick peas
asparagus spears
dried mushrooms
canned fish: sardines (they
    can be dipped in batter and
    deep-fried
for fritters), shrimp,
    salmon, tuna, anchovies,
    crab meat
canned ham
canned smoked oysters
canned mushrooms
canned stewed tomatoes
marinated artichokes, in jar
marinated mushrooms, in jar
chipped beef, in jar
pimiento, in jar
popover mix
mayonnaise
canned plum pudding
canned pâté
instant espresso
spiced peaches

Refrigerator

tubes of buttermilk biscuits
eggs
cheese
anchovy paste
cream cheese
sour cream

Freezer

chicken breasts
hamburger patties
chopped green pepper
chopped onions
pie shells
peeled uncooked shrimp
bread and rolls
fried crêpes
bulk pork sausage
butter
flavored butters

assorted vegetables
berries
casseroles
cream puff shells
patty shells
homemade soups
frozen whipped cream
   topping
angel food cake
pound cake
homemade pesto sauce

RECIPES

The recipes and entertaining information that follow are divided into sections for different types of parties. The order in which they appear roughly follows the progression of the clock. Brunches and Luncheons first, then The Tea Party, followed by Cocktails and Buffets, Picnics and Barbecues, and finally Dinner Parties. The final segment, Accompaning Recipes, is used to supplement these and your own favorite recipes. You will find some dependable classics here, but most of the dishes have a touch of the unexpected.

Brunches and Luncheons

Recently the weekend brunch has skyrocketed in popularity all across the country as a form of entertaining. An at-home brunch is one of the easiest and least expensive meals you can offer to guests. Meat and fish play relatively minor roles in the menu; the emphasis is more on eggs, cheeses, and breads.

The spirit of a brunch is so relaxed that I feel it is best not to have a planned seating arrangement. You may indicate where you will sit and let others place themselves where they like. Planned seating is more usual for a luncheon.

Unless you are the kind of person who wakes up bright-eyed and bouncy, prepare as much of the menu as possible the night before. Also set the table, check the bar, and give the house a quick once-over (leave the last-minute touches in the bathroom till morning).

For a large buffet you will need chafing dishes and/or electric warming trays.

Brunch or lunch can easily stretch into a long, lazy afternoon, which provides the perfect occasion for experimenting with unusual alcoholic and nonalcoholic beverages. Bloody Marys and Mimosas are popular choices, but instead of champagne, why not try a fruity white wine such as a Mosel from Germany or a Sylvaner from Al-

sace. *A good California Zinfandel would not be out of place either. You might try a punch based on sparkling wine, or some hot mulled wine on a chilly afternoon. If you can't decide whether your budget is beer poor or champagne rich, pour them both and enjoy a Black Velvet.*

A Sunday afternoon is also a perfect time to discover why the soda fountain of yesteryear was such a popular institution. Offer ice cream sodas and milk shakes and watch your guests' eyes light up.

Whatever else you are planning for dessert, provide some fresh fruit for your guests who would rather eat lightly at midday. Coffee should be plentiful and strong, of course, but don't forget your tea-drinking friends.

This first chapter of recipes concentrates for the most part on the main course. A few standbys and favorites are included; however, you will not find eggs benedict here or even plain scrambled eggs, but rather Stilton Tart, Parsley Pâté, Sour Cream Ramekin, and Gratin of Mussels and Spinach.

Yes, eggs figure importantly in this chapter, but when the eggs are scrambled, they are then mixed with kiwi puree—guaranteed to wake up sleepy guests. In another unusual presentation, scrambled eggs are mixed with raw eggs and turned into a mold for baking, resulting in a bright and mellow ring. Fish at lunch is not unexpected, but Crab Tart at brunch will certainly get noticed, as would Crêpes with Roquefort.

Since I felt it would be more useful to stress the wide variety of possibilities for the main course, recipes to round out the meal are very limited. Appetizers, vegetables, and desserts can be borrowed from other sections or from your own files.

Recipes have been selected with advance preparation in mind. Even the base for a soufflé can be cooked the day before and refrigerated, leaving only the egg whites to be beaten and added to the rewarmed sauce. It is hoped that the recipes that follow will help start off the day with a sparkling good time.

CURRIED FRUIT SOUP

Curried Fruit Soup will awaken jaded appetites on even the hottest summer day. It is a haunting, carefully balanced blend of spice, fruit, and vegetable flavors. Since the potato and bananas give the soup plenty of body, you can trim calories by substituting milk for the cream.

Serves 8

2 cups chicken broth
2 apples (MacIntosh or Stayman), peeled, cored, and cut
   into chunks
1 pound bananas, peeled and cut into chunks
1 potato, peeled and cut into chunks
1 small onion, peeled and cut into chunks
2 or 3 teaspoons curry powder
1 pint light cream
Garnish: grated lemon rind or grated apple mixed with
   lemon juice

1. Heat the chicken broth in a 2-quart pot. Add the apples, bananas, potato, and onion. Cover and simmer until soft, 15 to 20 minutes.

2. Transfer the cooked fruits and vegetables to a blender or food processer. Add curry; the exact amount will depend on your taste for curry and the strength of the brand you use, but keep in mind that when served cold the intensity of the curry flavor will soften. Puree until smooth, add cream and process for several seconds more. Pour into a bowl and chill thoroughly. Serve plain or garnished with the grated lemon rind or the grated apple (it should be tossed with lemon juice to keep it from discoloring).

STILTON TART

This recipe is based on one from a restaurant in Bath, England. Although this area is best known for cheddar cheese, some very good Stilton is also produced there.

Makes 1 deep 9-inch tart

    1 pound Sour Cream Pastry (page 248)
    5 eggs
    ¼ cup minced shallots
    10 ounces Stilton Cheese
    6 slices bacon, fried and crumbled
    2 tomatoes, peeled
    2 cups light cream
    ¼ teaspoon cayenne
    pepper
    2 teaspoons brandy

Preheat oven to 375 degrees.

1. Select a deep 9-inch pie pan and line it with the pastry. Put a piece of wax paper or foil in the lined pie dish and fill it with dried beans or weights. Bake for 15 minutes; remove the paper and beans or weights. Reduce the oven temperature to 375. Beat 1 egg with 1 tablespoon water and brush over the pastry; reserve any leftover egg wash. Return the pie shell to the oven for about 2 minutes, long enough to allow the egg wash to set into a glaze. (This glaze helps prevent the crust from becoming soggy when filled with the custard mixture.) Let cool.

2. Sprinkle the shallots over the bottom of the pastry shell, then crumble in the Stilton and bacon. Cut the tomatoes into thin slices and make a layer of them over the cheese. Beat together the remaining 4 eggs, cream, and any reserved egg wash; season with the cayenne, pepper, and brandy. Do not use any salt since the bacon and cheese are already salty. Pour the egg and cream mixture over the tart. Bake for about 45

minutes or until the custard has set and the top has puffed a little and is lightly browned. Check the consistency of the custard by inserting a thin knife into it; it should come out clean. Cool the tart for 10 minutes before serving.

CRÊPES WITH ROQUEFORT

When Salvador Dali arrived in America in 1940, he was already a celebrity, both as an artist and an eccentric. His every word was recorded. What did he think of New York? "It's a Gothic Roquefort." With that enigmatic statement, Roquefort was on its way to fame on these shores. True Roquefort is made of ewe's milk and comes from a village of that name in south-central France. No other blue-veined cheese can be called Roquefort, but other similar cheeses certainly can be used in these crêpes.

Serves 6

8 ounces Roquefort
3 tablespons heavy cream
2 teaspoons brandy
12 crêpes (page 246)
2 tablespoons grated Swiss cheese

Preheat oven to 350 degrees.
1. Using a fork, cream together the Roquefort, cream, and brandy. Spread the filling over each crêpe, roll, seam side down, and place the crêpes in a buttered baking dish. Sprinkle with the grated cheese. (This much of the preparation can be done well in advance.)
2. Bake for about 10 minutes or until the crêpes begin to turn a dark golden color. Serve immediately.

COTTAGE CHEESE PIE

The role of cottage cheese at lunch is usually restricted to the dieter's plate. This is regrettable since it can be used to make delicious and nutritious dishes at very little cost. Here is just one example.

Serves 6

1 8-inch pie shell (pages 247–48), partially baked
2 cups creamed cottage cheese
6 tablespoons yogurt
2 scallions including green tops, finely chopped
freshly grated nutmeg
salt and pepper
3 eggs, well beaten
¼ cup grated Parmesan cheese

Preheat oven to 375 degrees.

1. Mix together in a bowl the cottage cheese, yogurt, scallions, nutmeg, salt, and pepper. Add the eggs and blend them in very well.

2. Pour this batter into the pie shell, sprinkle with Parmesan cheese, and bake for about 35 minutes or until the pie is puffed and nicely browned. Allow to cool for 10 minutes before serving.

QUICHE LORRAINE

Quiche Lorraine has become almost a culinary cliché. Still, it is one of the most popular of all quiches, and deservedly so. My own version differs a little from most, but I wouldn't make it any other way.

Makes 1 10-inch quiche: serves 8

Pastry (pages 247–48) with 1 teaspoon each dry mustard
and paprika added to the flour
prepared mustard
10 to 12 slices bacon
1 pint milk
¼ pound Gruyere or Emmenthal cheese, cut into thin
slices
2 eggs
1 egg yolk
2 tablespoons heavy cream
salt and pepper
freshly grated nutmeg
¼ cup grated Parmesan cheese

1. Partially bake the pie shell according to the directions on pages 247–48. Remove from the oven and remove the weights and paper or foil, then paint with the prepared mustard and return to the oven for 5 minutes, with the heat on. Remove again from oven and reduce temperature to 350 degrees.

2. Over low heat, fry the bacon very well and drain between paper towels. Put the milk in a pot and slowly bring to the boiling point. Meanwhile, place the cheese slices in the bottom of the pie shell, and in a bowl beat together the eggs, egg yolk, cream, just a pinch of salt, and a good grinding of pepper. Slowly whisk in the hot milk. Crumble the bacon and add it to the bowl along with nutmeg. Don't be timid with the nutmeg; you should use enough that you can almost smell it.

3. Place the quiche shell on a baking pan with edges and ladle in most of the filling. Place the baking pan in the oven, ladle in the remainder of the filling, and sprinkle with the Parmesan cheese. Bake for about ½ hour or until a sharp knife plunged in the center comes out clean and almost dry. Cool the quiche for 10 minutes before cutting.

TARTE À L'OIGNON (ONION TART)

An Onion Tart is not a fearsome thing, even at brunch or lunch. The very long, very slow cooking reduces the seemingly large quantity of onions to a sweet, limp mass and the custard filling holds the strands all together. A thin wedge of Onion Tart could also start off a dinner, especially if followed by fish. You can also adapt the recipe to turn out individual tartlets to serve as an accompaniment to a roast.

Serves 6

> 1 8-inch partially baked pie shell (pages 247–48)
> 2 pounds onions, thinly sliced (about 7 cups)
> ¼ cup garlic-flavored or plain olive oil
> 1 garlic clove, minced
> 1 bay leaf
> 1 teaspoon meat extract, or ¼ cup meat gravy or roast juices
> salt and pepper
> 3 tablespoons flour
> 2 eggs or 3 egg yolks
> ⅓ cup heavy cream
> 1 teaspoon salt
> ¼ teaspoon pepper
> large pinch nutmeg
> ½ cup grated Swiss cheese (or half Swiss and half Parmesan)

1. In a heavy pot heat the oil over low heat. Add the onions and stir well until they are coated with oil. Cover pot tightly and simmer over very low heat for 15 minutes. Add the garlic and bay leaf and mix well again. Keep covered and simmer very slowly, stirring frequently so onions cook evenly. This will take at least 45 minutes. Onions should reduce greatly and become almost a pulp, but do not mash; you should be able to define the strands of golden onions. (The secret here is the

heavy pot and the slow cooking, which removes any suggestion of strong or bitter flavor.)

2. Remove the bay leaf and add the meat extract or meat juice (this helps to give a nice brown color to the onions) and salt and pepper to taste. Sprinkle the flour over the onions, mix well, cover, and simmer another 10 minutes. Let cool slightly. (The onions can be cooked well ahead of time, even the day before, and refrigerated. If they are refrigerated, reheat slowly before continuing.)

Preheat oven to 375 degrees.

3. Beat the eggs or egg yolks with the cream, teaspoon salt, 1/4 teaspoon pepper, and nutmeg (don't be afraid of overdoing the nutmeg). Mix in the lukewarm—not hot—onions and half the cheese; check the seasonings. Pour the mixture into the partially baked pie shell, sprinkle the rest of the cheese on top, and bake for 25 to 30 minutes. To check whether the tart is done, plunge a small sharp knife in the center; it should come out almost dry. The tart should be nicely browned and puffy. Let cool 5 minutes before serving.

RICE CROQUETTES WITH CHEESE SAUCE

Time was when croquettes of many flavorings were very popular. Today one rarely sees them except for an occasional limp example on a cafeteria steam table. Perhaps our current infatuation with foreign cooking has overshadowed this old American standby. When properly made, croquettes are very tasty and worth a reintroduction to the brunch or lunch table.

Serves 4

1 tablespoon butter
1 tablespoon flour
½ cup milk
large pinch of nutmeg
salt and pepper to taste
2 cups cooked rice
2 ounces ham, sausage, or other cooked meat, diced
2 teaspoons chopped dill
1 teaspoon salt
2 eggs
bread crumbs

Cheese Sauce:
   2 tablespoons butter
   2 tablespoons flour
   1 cup milk
   1 teaspoon Worcestershire sauce
   dash of Tabasco
   salt and pepper
   ¼ pound grated sharp cheddar cheese

   oil for frying

1. Melt the butter in a small saucepan, stir in the flour, and cook for half a minute. Slowly whisk in the milk and season with nutmeg, salt, and pepper.
2. In a mixing bowl, combine the rice, white sauce you've

just made, meat, dill, teaspoon salt, and eggs. Thoroughly blend all ingredients and flavorings. Chill for 15 to 30 minutes.

3. Spread the bread crumbs on a sheet of waxed paper or a large plate. Shape about 2 heaping tablespoons of the rice mixture into an oblong roll, then coat well with the bread crumbs. Place the breaded rolls on a baking sheet and chill for at least 1 hour. There should be 8 croquettes.

4. While the croquettes are chilling, prepare the sauce. In a saucepan, melt the butter, stir in the flour, and cook on low heat for 1 minute. Remove the pan from the heat and slowly stir in the milk with a wire whisk. Return to the heat and stir in the Worcestershire sauce, Tabasco, salt, and pepper. Finally, add the cheese, reduce heat to low, and stirring occasionally, allow the cheese to melt. Cover and set aside.

5. At serving time, pour enough oil into a deep-fryer or a large, flat-bottomed skillet to reach a depth of 1 inch. Heat the oil and when it is hot, add as many croquettes as will fit without crowding. Fry until delicately brown on all surfaces; this should take only a minute or so. Drain on paper towels, and place in a warm oven while frying the remaining croquettes.

6. While frying the croquettes, slowly reheat the cheese sauce. Serve both croquettes and sauce as hot as possible.

PARSLEY PÂTÉ

This delicately scented pâté has a very clean and pleasant aftertaste. It should star by itself and not compete with spicy accompaniments. A few sliced tomatoes will complete the picture-pretty effect of the white pâté studded with green parsley and bright carrot bits. It makes a perfect and unusual main course for lunch and especially for brunch. Have all ingredients thoroughly chilled, as well as the bowl of the food processor; this is necessary to produce the proper texture for the pâté.

Makes 2³/₄ pounds

1 small carrot
2 slices white bread, crusts removed
½ cup milk
1½ pounds skinless, boneless chicken breast, cut into
    1-inch pieces and chilled
1 teaspoon tarragon
½ teaspoon ground coriander
salt and pepper
2 egg whites
2 teaspoons aromatic bitters
2 cups heavy cream
2 cups parsley leaves, firmly packed

1. Cut the carrot into very small dice, about ⅛ inch square. Boil for about 2 minutes or until barely tender, drain, cool under cold running water, and drain well again. There should be about ½ cup carrot pieces. Chill the carrots on a dish lined with a paper towel and with another towel on top.

2. Chill the food processor bowl in the refrigerator and the steel blade in the freezer.

Preheat the oven to 325 degrees.

3. Tear the bread into pieces and soak in the milk for about 5 minutes. Put the chicken pieces in the chilled processor bowl and squeeze out the bread and add it to the bowl. Sprinkle in the tarragon, coriander, salt, and pepper and process with the on/off switch until the chicken is coarsely chopped.

4. Lightly beat the egg whites and bitters together and, with the motor running, pour into the processor. Scrape down the sides and, again with the motor running, pour in the cream. Add the parsley leaves and process very briefly, just enough to incorporate the parsley into the mousseline. Poach a spoonful of the mousseline in a little boiling water, cool, and taste for seasonings; correct if necessary. Sprinkle the carrot dice over the pâté mixture and work in lightly with a rubber spatula.

5. Cut two pieces of parchment paper to fit the bottom and top of a 6-cup mold. Butter the mold, lay one piece of parchment paper in the bottom, and butter it. Scoop the parsley mousseline into the mold and smooth its surface with a rubber

spatula. Tap the mold sharply on the counter a few times. Butter the other piece of parchment paper and lay it over the mousseline, greased side down. Cover the mold closely with aluminum foil and with a lid, if the mold has one. Poke a hole in the aluminum foil. Place the mold in a deep baking pan and pour in enough water to reach two-thirds of the way up the sides of the mold. Bake for 30 to 40 minutes or until a meat thermometer registers 140 degrees.

6. Remove the lid and the foil, but leave the mold in the water bath for 30 minutes. Then weight the top lightly, using no more than 2 pounds. Remove the weights after 2 hours. Chill the pâté for 2 or 3 days. Remove from the refrigerator about 1 hour before serving.

SPAGHETTI WITH PARSLEY SAUCE

This spaghetti with its delicate coating should definitely be served at the beginning of a dinner rather than as the main course. Its very delicacy of flavor and unsaucelike appearance also make it an unusual main dish for weekend brunches. You should have most of the ingredients already on hand.

Serves 6 as a first course

3 tablespoons oil
1 tablespoon salt
1 pound spaghetti
½ cup butter
2 garlic cloves, minced
¼ cup grated Parmesan cheese; extra cheese optional
salt and pepper
3 cups roughly chopped parsley leaves

1. Bring about 4 quarts of water to a boil and add 2 tablespoons of oil and 1 tablespoon salt. Add the spaghetti slowly to maintain the rolling boil and cook uncovered for about 7

minutes or just until *al dente*. Drain at once and shake the colander vigorously to extrude as much water as possible.

2. While the spaghetti is cooking, melt butter with the remaining tablespoon of oil in a large, flat, preferably heavy skillet. Add the garlic and simmer just half a minute while stirring with a wooden spoon. Add the cooked spaghetti, Parmesan cheese, a little salt, and a generous grinding of pepper and toss well to coat all the spaghetti strands with the butter. Cover, reduce heat, and reheat for 1 minute. Turn off the heat, add the parsley, and toss well. Transfer the spaghetti to a deep, warmed serving bowl. (The plates should also be warm.) Pass the optional extra Parmesan cheese.

GRIBI C SMETANOI (MUSHROOM AND SOUR CREAM RAMEKIN)

I first enjoyed this Russian dish when I lived in Moscow. *Gribi* means mushrooms; usually pungent wild varieties are used. For *smetanoi* (sour cream) I went to the farmers market and sampled from several buckets before making a selection. The health department would blanch, but I never tasted better. The addition of lemon juice and Parmesan cheese to this recipe helps recapture some of the original flavor. This is a dish you will use often. For lunch either bake it in small gratin dishes or serve on toast. A small custard cup of it does nicely as a first course for dinner.

Serves 6

½ cup butter
1 cup chopped onion
1 pound mushrooms, sliced
3 tablespoons flour
2 cups sour cream
juice of ½ lemon
2 teaspoons salt
pepper
¼ cup grated Parmesan cheese

1. Melt the butter in a large heavy skillet. Add the onions, cover, and simmer about 10 minutes or until the onions are soft.

2. Add the mushrooms, cover, and cook for 5 minutes. Reduce the heat and sprinkle in the flour. Mix thoroughly to distribute the flour and cook for about 1 minute, stirring constantly. Remove the skillet from the heat and stir in the sour cream, lemon juice, salt, and pepper. Return to the heat and cook 2 minutes more. (The dish can be prepared to this point in advance and refrigerated.)

Preheat oven to 375 degrees.

3. Spoon the mushroom mixture into a 10-inch pie dish or 6 individual gratin dishes and sprinkle with Parmesan cheese. Bake for 10 to 15 minutes or until the sauce bubbles and the top is lightly browned.

CORN FRITTERS

These corn fritters are a more delicate version of the popular American classic. The difference lies in using a minimal amount of batter to bind the kernels and the addition of lots of freshly grated nutmeg. Finally, the fritters are sautéed in a small amount of butter rather than fried in a large amount of oil. Small adjustments, but a big improvement in the final product. Serve as a main course at brunch with grilled tomatoes and fried mushrooms.

Makes 14 to 16 fritters

2 eggs
2 1-pound cans whole kernel corn, preferably
   vacuum-packed
½ teaspoon salt
½ teaspoon freshly grated nutmeg
½ cup flour
2 tablespoons oil (approximately)
3 tablespoons butter (approximately)

1. Put the eggs in the jar of a blender. If the corn is not vacuum-packed, drain well. Add the corn to the blender and process on low speed for only a few seconds. The mixture should not be smooth; in fact, it is better to leave a few whole kernels to give a nice firmness to the fritters. Scoop the corn into a mixing bowl and add the salt and nutmeg.

2. Add the flour, mix well, and let the mixture stand for at least 15 minutes to allow the flour to absorb the liquid.

3. In a large heavy skillet, heat a little of the oil and 3 tablespoons of butter. The fat should not be deep but should generously coat the bottom of the skillet. When the fat is hot, spoon in 2 tablespoons of the batter for each fritter and flatten them with the back of a spoon. Do not crowd fritters in the pan or they will not brown evenly and will be difficult to turn. Fry them until nicely browned on one side, then turn and fry the other side.

4. Remove the fritters to drain on absorbent paper and keep them warm while cooking the rest of the batter. Add more oil and butter to the skillet as necessary.

SUNBURST SALAD

This is an ambitious and stunning salad with a base of plain old rice transformed by a real glamour treatment. A summer luncheon is the obvious setting for it, but any buffet table would also be enhanced by Sunburst Salad.

Serves 8 to 10 as a main course

Rice Salad:
   4 cups boiled rice
   1 cup diced, cooked green beans
   1 cup diced, cooked carrots
   1 cup peeled, diced cucumber
   1 cup peeled, diced tomatoes
   ½ cup ham, diced

½ cup cooked tongue, diced
1 cup French dressing
1 large bunch watercress

1. In a large bowl combine all rice salad ingredients except French dressing and watercress. Pour the dressing over and mix lightly. Put the salad in a shallow wooden or silver bowl. Make a hole in the center and fill it with the watercress. Refrigerate while preparing the stuffed eggs.

Stuffed Eggs:

8 hard-boiled eggs
½ cup butter
¼ to ⅓ cup pesto (pages 244–45)
½ cup cream cheese
2 tablespoons tomato paste
2 teaspoons tomato ketchup
2 teaspoons Worcestershire sauce
salt and cayenne pepper
capers and basil leaves for garnish
2 peeled tomatoes

2. Cut the eggs in half lengthwise. Carefully scoop out the yolks, drop them into a sieve or strainer, and work them through. Cream the butter and add it to the yolks. Divide the mixture in half. Stir pesto into one half, using enough to achieve a bright green color. Mix the other portion with the cream cheese, tomato paste, tomato ketchup, Worcestershire sauce, salt, and cayenne.

3. Fill half the egg-white halves with the rose-colored filling and the other half with the green. Squeezing the filling through a pastry bag gives the prettiest effect, but it may be scooped in with a teaspoon.

4. Arrange the stuffed eggs in alternating flavors around the edge of the rice salad with the smaller ends pointing toward the center. Decorate each rose-colored egg with capers and each pesto egg with basil leaves. Cut the 2 tomatoes into eighths and tuck slices between the eggs, also pointing toward the center. Chill until ready to serve.

SCRAMBLED EGGS WITH KIWI

Nouvelle cuisine made a star of kiwi, but usually emphasizes its decorative nature and not its flavor. But flavor it has in plenty, plus a little string of tartness. Combining its acid freshness with rich foods can produce some stunning combinations. I find soft scrambled eggs one such match. Using kiwi shells to hold the cooked eggs makes the prettiest presentation, but there will be more filling than shells. So a day or so before your party, enjoy some of the fruit plain and save the shells by refrigerating them in a plastic bag.

Serves 6

3 kiwis
3 tablespoons butter
9 eggs, beaten
salt and pepper
toast
1 kiwi (optional for garnish)

1. Cut the 3 kiwis in half lengthwise. With a teaspoon, carefully scoop the flesh into a bowl. Snip off the hard inside stem end of the fruit with small scissors. Mash the kiwi pulp with a fork. If it seems excessively watery, press some of the juice out, but usually this is not necessary.

2. Melt the butter in a heavy saucepan placed on a heat-deflector pad or in the top of a double boiler suspended above the water, not in it. To cook soft, creamy scrambled eggs, the heat must be kept low for slow cooking. Add the eggs and, stirring constantly, cook until they take on shape but are not hard curds. This may take 15 minutes. Season with salt and pepper.

3. Stir the crushed kiwi fruit into the eggs, mixing well. Cook another minute or so to warm up the fruit. Spoon the eggs into the kiwi shells, allowing 2 or 3 shells per serving, or serve on warmed shallow dishes. Peel and slice an additional kiwi and garnish each portion with a slice, if desired. Serve with warm toast.

EGG-AND-ONION TARTLETS

The slow, gentle sautéing of the onions is important in turning them into sweet shreds that blend well with the eggs. Individual tartlets are the prettiest presentation, but an 8-inch pie shell may also be used.

Serves 6

1¼ pounds pastry (pages 247–48)
2 medium onions, very thinly sliced
3 tablespoons butter
10 eggs
salt and pepper
Tabasco
2 tablespoons heavy cream
2 tablespoons butter, diced (optional)
minced parsley

Preheat oven to 375 degrees.

1. Roll out the pastry and cut into 6 4-inch rounds. Fit the pastry into 6 individual 3 ½-inch tartlet pans, pushing the dough into the fluted sides so that it will take on that form and pushing the dough lightly upward to create a deeper shell. Prick each shell bottom with a small, sharp knife. Line each tart pan with parchment paper and fill with dry beans or other weights. Bake for 10 minutes or until the edges begin to brown slightly. Remove from the oven, scoop out the beans, discard the paper, prick the shells again, and return them to the oven. Turn off the heat and finish baking the shells for another 5 minutes. Remove shells from the pans.

2. In a heavy pan melt the butter, then add the onions. Cover and cook over very low heat until the onions turn very soft and sweet, about 30 minutes. Stir often, and do not allow them to brown. (This step may be done well in advance.)

3. At serving time, beat the eggs together with salt, pepper, and a good dash of Tabasco. If onions have cooled, place the

pan containing them on a heat-deflector pad and reheat the onions. Stir in the eggs and keep stirring constantly until they are set. Remove the pan from the heat and stir in the cream and the optional butter if desired, mixing until they are completely absorbed. Immediately spoon the egg and onion mixture into the pastry shells, sprinkle with parsley, and serve at once.

BAKED NEAPOLITAN EGG MOLD

Serving hot egg dishes usually means that the cook must be in the kitchen at the last minute. Here is one very eggy presentation that is prepared almost entirely in advance (even the day before, if you like) and then baked. The egg filling—a combination of lightly scrambled and raw eggs—can be baked in individual *baba* molds or in a ring mold. A tomato sauce spooned over the top gives the dish a Neapolitan touch.

Serves 6

14 eggs
¼ teaspoon Tabasco
1 teaspoon ground pepper
large pinch of salt
3 to 4 tablespoons butter
1 cup grated Parmesan cheese
Tomato Sauce (page 244)

1. Break 6 eggs into a bowl and beat lightly. Season with Tabasco, pepper, and pinch of salt. Set aside.
2. Melt 2 tablespoons of butter in a heavy copper or enameled cast-iron skillet. Break remaining 8 eggs into another bowl and beat lightly with a fork. Pour them into the skillet, reduce the heat to low, and begin stirring with a wooden spatula. Keep

stirring and scraping the bottom of the skillet to pull up the almost-cooked eggs into the liquid eggs. The consistency must remain custardy and without any hard-cooked curds. If necessary, place a heat-deflector pad under the skillet to keep the heat low enough. This preliminary cooking will take about 15 minutes, with constant attention. When finished, the eggs should resemble a lumpy Hollandaise. Remove from the heat.

3. Immediately stir the seasoned raw-egg mixture into the cooked eggs, thus stopping any further cooking. Add ¾ cup of the cheese and stir well.

4. Select either 6 1-cup molds or a 6-cup ring mold and butter liberally. Sprinkle each mold with the remaining Parmesan cheese and rotate to coat the entire surface; pour out any excess cheese. Chill molds for 30 minutes to harden the butter and set the cheese. Carefully ladle the egg custard into the molds. (The dish can be refrigerated at this point.)

Preheat oven to 350 degrees.

5. Place the mold in a pan and fill pan with enough hot water to reach halfway up the sides of the mold. Bake for about 30 minutes or until a knife inserted into the custard comes out clean. (If undercooked, the baked eggs will collapse when being unmolded.)

6. Allow the mold to stand for 2 minutes, then cut around it and reverse onto a warm serving platter. Spoon a little hot tomato sauce over the egg mold and pass the rest of the sauce at the table.

ASPARAGUS SOUFFLÉ

Now that the season for fresh asparagus stretches far beyond springtime, this impressive soufflé can be enjoyed often. Broiled tomatoes with a dribble of olive oil and a few bread crumbs scattered over the top are a nice balancing note.

Serves 4 to 5

1 pound asparagus
3 tablespoons butter
2 tablespoons flour
½ cup milk
4 eggs, separated
¼ cup grated Swiss cheese
large pinch of nutmeg
few drops of Tabasco
salt and pepper
pinch of cream of tartar

1. Snap off the tough, woody ends of the asparagus and, using a swivel-bladed vegetable peeler, peel away the tough skin of the stalks. Lay the asparagus in a flat skillet. Pour in ¼ inch of water, bring the water to a boil, cover, and cook briskly for about 2 or 3 minutes or until the asparagus is just tender. Remove the asparagus at once and reserve ½ cup of the cooking liquid.

Preheat oven to 400 degrees.

2. Cut off 4 asparagus tips and reserve. Cut the remaining stalks into pieces and puree in a blender or food processor. In a saucepan melt 2 tablespoons of butter until foamy; stir in the flour and cook for 1 minute. Mixing with a wire whisk, pour in the reserved cooking liquid and the milk. Cook over moderate heat for about 5 minutes or until the sauce has thickened.

3. Remove the saucepan from the heat and beat in the egg yolks one at a time. Add the asparagus puree, cheese, nutmeg, Tabasco, salt, and pepper.

4. Beat the egg whites until soft and foamy; add the cream of tartar and beat until stiff. Fold a third of the beaten whites into the soufflé base and mix delicately but well to lighten the thick sauce. Carefully fold in the remaining egg whites, but do not overmix and cause the egg whites to break down.

5. Use the remaining tablespoon of butter to grease a 6-cup soufflé dish. Carefully pour in the batter and smooth the top. Run your thumb around the inside of the rim and remove about a quarter of an inch of the batter. This will help produce a high-rising center hat on the soufflé. Garnish the center with the 4 reserved asparagus tips. Place in the oven, reduce the heat to

375 degrees, and bake for about 30 minutes or until the top is browned and puffed up. Serve immediately.

CHEESE SOUFFLÉ *EXTRAORDINAIRE*

This soufflé is delicate, but that doesn't mean fragile. Flour has been replaced by cornstarch in this recipe and the resulting puff of goodness lacks the heavy starchy flavor that flour usually produces. The method for making the sauce is also different—and foolproof.

Serves 6 to 8

4 tablespoons butter, at room temperature
2 cups heavy cream
2 tablespoons cornstarch
½ pound Swiss cheese, grated
¼ cup grated Parmesan cheese
nutmeg
large pinch cayenne
salt and pepper
6 eggs, separated
pinch of cream of tartar
3 very thin slices sharp cheddar cheese

Preheat oven to 375 degrees.

1. Use 1 tablespoon of butter to grease a 2-quart soufflé dish. In a saucepan heat 1½ cups of the cream and the remaining 3 tablespoons of butter until the butter melts. Meanwhile, stir the remaining ½ cup of cream into the cornstarch to make a thin paste. Add the cornstarch paste to the hot cream and continue cooking and stirring until the sauce thickens. Remove from the heat and let cool for 5 minutes.

2. Stir in the Swiss and Parmesan cheeses and season with nutmeg, cayenne, pepper, and very little salt since the cheeses are salty. Beat the egg yolks and add them to the cheese base. (The sauce can be prepared to this stage several hours or even

a day in advance and refrigerated. Reheat slowly to just lukewarm before continuing.)

3. Beat the egg whites until quite firm; if not using a copper bowl, add a pinch of cream of tartar to the whites once they are soft and foamy. Scoop a third of the beaten whites over the cheese sauce and fold them in quite thoroughly using a wire whisk. Scrape the remaining whites over the soufflé sauce and lightly fold them in with a rubber spatula. Do not overmix.

4. Pour the soufflé mixture into the prepared mold. Cut the cheddar cheese slices into diamonds or triangles and arrange them in the center of the soufflé. Bake for about 30 minutes or until the top is puffed and nicely browned. Serve at once, using two spoons for separating the soufflé into portions.

ROLLED SPINACH OMELET

This spinach roll is a cross between an omelet and a soufflé, without either the last-minute flurry of the former or the delicate temperament of the latter. Fillings of all sorts can be used: crab meat, plain or smoked salmon in a fish velouté sauce, mushrooms and tomatoes in a white sauce, chicken with peas and sautéed onions in a brown sauce, and on and on.

Serves 6 to 8

Omelet Roll:
    4 tablespoons butter
    ½ cup flour
    2 cups milk
    ½ teaspoon salt
    large pinch of pepper
    dash Tabasco
    5 eggs, separated
    large pinch cream of tartar
    2 tablespoons grated Parmesan cheese
    ½ cup bread crumbs

Filling:
>   2 tablespoons butter
>   3 shallots, finely chopped
>   1 cup chopped mushrooms
>   1 cup cooked, well-drained spinach, chopped
>   4 slices boiled ham, diced
>   1 tablespoon prepared mustard
>   ½ teaspoon nutmeg
>   6 ounces cream cheese, broken into chunks
>   salt and pepper
>   ¼ cup milk (optional)

Preheat oven to 400 degrees.

1. Butter a jelly roll pan measuring approximately 15½ x 10½ x 1 inch. Line the pan with a sheet of parchment paper long enough to extend beyond the pan by several inches on each side; butter the parchment paper. (Note: Wax paper does not work nearly as well as parchment paper because it has a tendency to stick to the baked omelet.)

2. To make the omelet, melt the 4 tablespoons of butter in a saucepan, blend in the flour, and cook until foamy. Slowly stir in the milk, then add the salt and pepper and a good dash of Tabasco. Cook for 1 minute or until the sauce is thick. In a small mixing bowl, beat the egg yolks; then, while continuing to beat, add a little of the hot sauce to the yolks. Return the sauce and yolks to the pot and cook over medium heat for 1 minute longer, stirring constantly. Do not allow the sauce to boil. Scrape the sauce into a large mixing bowl and set it aside to cool for 5 minutes. Stir the sauce occasionally as it cools.

3. Add the cream of tartar to softly beaten egg whites and beat until stiff. Scoop a third of the beaten whites into the cooled sauce and fold them in thoroughly with a whisk. Scrape in the remaining whites and gently fold them into the mixture with a rubber spatula; do not overwork the whites or they will break down. Pour the omelet mixture into the prepared jelly roll pan and spread it to form an even layer. Sprinkle with the Parmesan cheese and bake for 15 to 20 minutes or until puffed and brown.

4. While the omelet is baking, prepare the filling. Melt the butter in a skillet, add the shallots, and simmer for 2 minutes. Add the mushrooms, cover, and cook over medium heat until they give up their moisture, about 2 or 3 minutes. Add the spinach, ham, mustard, and nutmeg; then stir in the cream cheese and cook over low heat until the cream cheese melts. Season to taste with salt and pepper. If the filling seems too thick to spread easily, add just enough milk to achieve the proper consistency. Cover the skillet and set aside.

5. Spread a clean dish towel on a flat surface and sprinkle with the bread crumbs. When the omelet is done, turn the pan over onto the dish towel; lift off the pan, then carefully pull away the parchment paper. Spread the spinach filling over the baked omelet. With the aid of the towel, roll the omelet into a long cylinder. Slide the omelet onto a serving platter, seam side down. Cut into slices with serrated knife, taking care not to press too heavily.

NOTE: This rolled omelet can also be served cold accompanied by a sauceboat of sour cream thinned with a little milk or mushroom cooking juices and seasoned with salt, pepper, and snipped dill.

ROULADE DE FROMAGES (CHEESE ROLL)

This cheese roll is a variation of the preceding rolled omelet. In this case, however, the filling requires no cooking. It is based on the soft French cheese sold under the names of Gervais or Boursault. Do not confuse this mild cheese with those that are flavored with herbs and spices.

Serves 6 to 8

Sauce:
    2 ounces salmon caviar
    2/3 cup sour cream
    1/4 teaspoon grated lemon rind

Roulade:

¼ cup butter, plus extra butter for greasing pan and
   paper
⅓ cup flour
¼ teaspoon salt
¼ teaspoon pepper
2 cups milk
4 eggs, separated
1 teaspoon sugar
pinch cream of tartar
1 tablespoon fine dry bread crumbs

Filling:

4 ounces Gervais, Boursin, or Boursault cheese
½ teaspoon finely chopped chives
¼ teaspoon lemon juice
4 ounces salmon caviar (not lumpfish)

Preheat oven to 350 degrees.

1. To prepare the sauce, force the 2 ounces of caviar through a sieve and then blend it into the sour cream. Stir in lemon rind. Chill.

2. Butter a 15½ x 10½ x 1-inch jelly roll pan and line it with parchment paper. Set aside. In a saucepan over low heat, melt ¼ cup butter; stir in the flour, salt, and pepper and cook until it is a smooth roux, about 2 minutes. Gradually add the milk and cook the sauce about 3 minutes, stirring constantly. Remove the pan from the heat. Add the egg yolks and sugar and beat the sauce thoroughly.

3. Beat the whites until they are soft and a little foamy, then add the cream of tartar and beat until the whites are stiff. With the wire whisk work about a third of the whites into the sauce, and then gently fold in the remaining whites with a rubber spatula; do not overmix and break down the whites. Spread the batter in the prepared pan and bake for about 30 minutes or until the egg sheet is well browned.

4. While the *roulade* is baking, prepare the filling. Mash the cheese with a fork to soften it. Blend in the chives and lemon

juice, and lastly fold in the caviar carefully so as not to crush the eggs.

5. Butter sheet of wax paper the same size as the baking sheet and sprinkle it with the bread crumbs. Turn the baked egg sheet onto the bread crumbs and peel off the paper from the baked sheet. Spread the surface with the caviar-cheese filling and roll up to make a 15-inch-long roll. Transfer to a serving platter, seam side down. Cut into 1-inch slices and pass the sauce separately. The *roulade* may be served hot or cold.

EGG CRÊPES WITH HAM

The thin pancakes used in this recipe are not flour-based crêpes but more closely resemble the flat Oriental omelet. In Oriental cooking the thin rounds are rolled and shredded to add visual interest to many dishes. I decided instead to use them in the manner of true crêpes.

Serves 4 to 6

3 eggs, at room temperature
1 tablespoon cornstarch
¼ cup milk
¼ cup water
2 tablespoons chopped basil
dash of Tabasco
salt and pepper
3 tablespoons butter (approximately)
12 thin slices slightly smoky-flavored ham
¼ cup sour cream
¾ cup heavy cream
2 tablespoons Parmesan cheese

1. Beat the eggs thoroughly. Mix the cornstarch with 1 or 2 tablespoons of water to make a paste and beat this paste into the eggs. Whisk in the milk and water and season with basil, a

good dash of Tabasco, pepper, and just a pinch of salt. There should be about 1 cup of batter.

2. In a 5- or 6-inch skillet or crêpe pan, melt about ¼ teaspoon butter. Rotate the skillet to grease the entire surface or spread the melted butter with a paper towel. When the skillet is hot, spoon in a scant 1½ tablespoons of the batter and quickly rotate the skillet to cover the entire surface with the batter; the omelet should be quite thin. When the bottom is lightly browned, slide the omelet out onto a dish without frying the other side. Continue making crêpes until all the batter is used. There should be about 12 crêpes.

Preheat oven to 400 degrees.

3. Butter a 9-inch pie dish or other gratin dish. Lay a slice of ham on the uncooked side of each egg crêpe, roll it up, and place crêpe in the dish seam-side down. Beat together the sour cream and heavy cream and pour over the crêpes. Sprinkle with the Parmesan cheese. Bake crêpes for 7 to 10 minutes or until some of the cream sauce has been absorbed and the top is lightly browned. Serve at once, allotting 2 or 3 crêpes to a serving depending on what else is being served.

TUNA-COTTAGE CHEESE CAKES

These tasty little cakes make an unexpected change of pace from usual luncheon fare. Another thing in their favor is that they are very good served cold, which means that the frying can be done the day before. When made bite-size, they are an admirable cocktail savory.

Serves 4

1 1-pound can tuna fish, packed in oil
½ cup creamed cottage cheese
1 medium onion, grated
½ cup fine bread crumbs
1 beaten egg
1 teaspoon soy sauce
¼ teaspoon salt
¼ teaspoon pepper
oil for frying
mayonnaise

1. Put the undrained tuna fish in a mixing bowl, add the cottage cheese, and mash the two together to achieve a smooth mixture. Add the grated onion, bread crumbs, egg, soy sauce, salt, and pepper. Mix thoroughly and let the mixture stand for at least 15 minutes.

2. Pour oil into a frying pan to a depth of ½ inch and heat it well. With your hands, pat about 3 tablespoons of the tuna mixture into a flat patty, not quite ½ inch thick. Carefully slip the patty into the oil and continue forming patties; there should be about 8. Fry the cakes for 2 or 3 minutes on each side until they are light brown; turn them carefully because they are delicate. Remove the fried cakes to a dish lined with paper towels and pat the tops with paper towels. Serve cakes lukewarm or cold; the flavor is not at its most delicate when hot. Serve with mayonnaise.

CRAB TART

A restrained amount of seasoning is used in this tart to allow the crab flavor to come through. The tart can be completely baked the day before the luncheon and reheated in a 325-degree oven for 20 minutes before serving.

Serves 4 to 6

1 partially baked 9-inch pastry shell (pages 247–48)
½ pound crab meat (fresh, canned, or frozen)
2 tablespoons shallots, finely chopped
2 tablespoons butter
2 tablespoons parsley, finely chopped
½ teaspoon tarragon
4 eggs
1½ cups heavy cream
2 tablespoons Madeira
salt and pepper
¼ cup grated Parmesan cheese

1. Simmer the chopped shallots in the butter for just a few minutes; they should be quite soft, but not brown. Put the crab meat in a mixing bowl, trying to keep the pieces as large as possible. Add the shallots to the crab along with the parsley, and tarragon.

2. In a separate bowl, beat together the eggs, cream, Madeira, salt and pepper, then gently fold this into the crab meat mixture. Spoon the filling into the tart shell and sprinkle with the Parmesan cheese. Bake for about 30 minutes or until the custard is set; a small sharp knife plunged into the center should come out almost dry. Serve hot, but not excessively hot.

MAKE-AHEAD CRAB CASSEROLE

Your nerves will always be calmed by advance preparations; the more the better. No compromises need be made for this casserole; in fact it is mandatory to prepare the dish at least 12 hours ahead of time. Only the baking is done the day of the meal.

Serves 8

3 tablespoons butter
½ cup mushrooms, sliced
2 tablespoons flour
1 cup light cream
salt and pepper
1 cup celery, chopped
8 slices soft white bread, crusts removed, diced
2 cups crab meat (fresh, canned, or frozen)
1 onion, chopped
½ cup mayonnaise
½ cup green pepper, chopped
½ cup almonds, blanched and slivered
4 eggs
3 cups milk
grated Parmesan cheese (approximately 3 tablespoons)
paprika

1. Melt 2 tablespoons of the butter in a small saucepan, add the mushrooms, and simmer them for 3 minutes, covered. Add the flour and mix well with a wooden spatula until the roux is foamy. Slowly pour in the cream while mixing with a wire whisk. Season with salt and pepper and put aside to cool, then refrigerate.
2. Cook the celery slowly for 10 minutes in a little water; drain well. Use the remaining tablespoon of butter to generously grease a 2-quart soufflé dish or one that's similar. Spread half the diced bread in the dish.

3. In a large bowl, lightly mix the picked-over crab meat, onion, mayonnaise, green pepper, half the almonds, and the celery. Spread this crab mixture evenly over the bread, then top with the remaining diced bread. Beat the eggs and milk together and pour over the contents of the dish. Cover and refrigerate overnight.
Preheat oven to 325 degrees.
4. Remove the crab dish and the prepared white sauce from the refrigerator 15 minutes before baking. Bake the casserole for 15 minutes, then spread the white sauce over the casserole and sprinkle with the grated cheese, paprika, and the remaining almonds. Bake 1 hour more, or until golden brown and puffy.

MUSSEL-AND-SPINACH GRATIN

There are no last-minute concerns about having this unconventional dish ready; all the preliminary steps can be done the day before. The sauce is best prepared just before baking, but it involves nothing more than combining a few ingredients.

Serves 4 to 6

    2 quarts mussels, steamed (pages 191–92)
    2½ cups cooked, squeezed, and chopped spinach
    ½ cup cooking liquor from steamed mussels
    1 cup heavy cream
    juice of ½ lemon
    salt and pepper
    1 teaspoon cornstarch
    3 teaspoons cold water
    ½ cup fine bread crumbs
    ½ cup grated Swiss cheese

Preheat oven to 400 degrees.
1. Remove the cooked mussels from their shells and combine them with the spinach. Carefully strain the mussel liquor

into a saucepan, add the cream, and bring to a simmer. Add the lemon juice, salt, and pepper and check seasonings. Mix the cornstarch with the cold water to make a thin paste and slowly add this paste to the hot sauce. Simmer for a minute or so until the sauce thickens a little.

2. Combine the sauce with the mussel-spinach mixture and pour into a greased baking dish. Sprinkle the bread crumbs and cheese on top and bake until the cheese melts and the crumbs are lightly browned, about 15 minutes. You may put it under the broiler for a short minute to give it a deeper color.

PLATTER FISH SOUFFLÉ

This low-rising soufflé puffs up nicely on a platter rather than shooting up dramatically in a mold. One small preliminary step is important to the success of the dish: the fish must be lightly poached, really just barely heated through. The French cooking term is *raidir*; it literally means "to stiffen." The purpose is to get the fish to give off its liquid. If not removed beforehand, the liquid will be exuded during the baking of the soufflé, resulting in a mess.

Serves 4

1 medium onion, thinly sliced
1 pound turbot, sole, or flounder fillets
salt and pepper
1 cup milk (approximately)
3 tablespoons butter
3 tablespoons flour
nutmeg
3 egg yolks
4 egg whites
pinch of cream of tartar
½ cup grated Swiss cheese

1. Scatter the onions in the bottom of a heavy, nonreactive pan. Place the fish fillets over the onions, skin-side underneath. Sprinkle with salt and pepper. Pour in cold milk, just

enough to barely cover the fillets. Cover tightly and bring to a simmer very slowly, then poach at this low heat just 1 minute. Remove the fillets from pan to cool. If you have thick fillets, cut them diagonally into scallops; otherwise leave the fillets whole. Cook the milk and onions together for 5 minutes, then strain the milk.

Preheat oven to 400 degrees.

2. In a heavy saucepan, heat the butter until foamy, then add the flour and cook while whisking for 1 minute. Add ¾ cup of milk, first using the reserved poaching milk and then adding more if necessary. Cook until the sauce is quite thick; add salt, pepper, and nutmeg. Off the heat, beat in the egg yolks; return the pan to the heat and give the sauce one good boil, then remove from heat.

3. Beat the egg whites until stiff, adding a pinch of cream of tartar once they are frothy. Add a quarter of the beaten whites to the sauce and blend well with the wire whisk. With a rubber spatula, fold in the rest of the egg whites and ¼ cup of the cheese.

4. Select on ovenproof rectangular or oval platter that is 12 to 14 inches long and 1 to 1½ inches deep. Butter the platter liberally. Spread half of the soufflé sauce in the platter and place the fish fillets over it but do not put them near the edge. Smooth the remaining sauce over the fish with a rubber spatula, then sprinkle on the remaining ¼ cup of cheese. Bake for 15 to 20 minutes or until the top has puffed and browned nicely. Serve at once.

NOTE: If you wish to serve a sauce with the soufflé, either a hollandaise or a mousseline may be used.

UNCOOKED APPLESAUCE

Light and refreshing—two words that are especially welcome at lunchtime. Both accurately describe this dessert.

Serves 5 to 6

¼ cup lemon juice
¼ cup orange juice
¼ cup white wine
2 tablespoons sugar or honey, or more to taste
⅛ teaspoon cinnamon
⅛ teaspoon nutmeg
4 apples

1. In the jar of a blender process together the lemon juice, orange juice, white wine, sugar or honey, cinnamon, and nutmeg.
2. Peel, quarter, and core the apples, then cut into chunks. Add the apple pieces to the blender and process to a puree. Taste for sweetness and flavorings and adjust if necessary. Serve at once, or cover tightly and refrigerate immediately.

PINEAPPLE WITH STRAWBERRY SAUCE

This refreshing dessert is simplicity itself, just two complementary fresh fruits chilled and served together. The success of the dish depends entirely on the quality of the fruits; the pineapple must be fresh and the sauce made of good ripe strawberries.

Serves 6

1½ pints strawberries
6 to 8 tablespoons sugar
1 teaspoon lemon juice
1 tablespoon orange liqueur or kirsch
6 slices fresh pineapple, about ¾ inch thick, chilled
6 mint sprigs

1. Put the strawberries, 6 tablespoons of sugar, lemon juice, and liqueur in the container of a blender or food processor.

Puree until smooth. Put the sauce aside and let sit at room temperature for 30 minutes. Taste for sugar and add the additional 2 tablespoons if necessary. Chill the sauce.

2. At serving time, pour ¼ cup of the sauce onto each individual dessert dish, preferably also chilled. Rotate the dish to create an even circle of the red sauce, place the pineapple slice in the center, and garnish with the mint sprig in the center.

STRAWBERRY SHERBET

Fresh fruit sherbets are a true culinary joy. As good as the fruit itself is, the sparkling icy mounds somehow are better still. Unlike ice creams, which benefit from ripening, I believe fruit sherbets should be served as soon after freezing as possible. The mixture can be made the day before and refrigerated, then frozen in the morning.

Serves 8

½ cup sugar
⅓ cup water
1 quart fresh strawberries
juice of 1 lemon
2 tablespoons orange liqueur, preferably Grand Marnier
1 egg white

1. In a small, heavy pot, bring the sugar and water to a boil. Simmer for 5 minutes and remove from the heat; cool.

2. Rinse and hull the berries. Place them in the container of a blender or food processor with the lemon juice and orange liqueur and puree. There should be about 3 cups of puree. Add the sugar syrup and blend again very briefly. Chill.

3. Lightly beat the egg white and pour it into the puree. Stir, but do not blend again. Pour the strawberry mixture into the container of an ice cream freezer and freeze according to the manufacturer's instructions. (If you lack an ice cream freezer,

pour the mixture into a 9-inch cake pan and place in the freezer. When the edges are frozen but the center is still soft, mix it all together into a mush and then refreeze. Repeat this one to two more times.)

NOTE: If the sherbet is made a day or more in advance, remove from the freezer 15 minutes before serving.

NECTARINE ICE CREAM

This is one of the easiest ice cream recipes you're likely to see. It should inspire the cook to try other flavors like peach or apricot. Use chilled ingredients when making ice cream so you can put the mixture in the freezer immediately. To speed up ice cream making, it's a good idea to prepare extra sugar syrup and store it in the refrigerator. It keeps indefinitely.

Serves 5 or 6

½ cup sugar
⅓ cup water
2 eggs
juice of 1 lemon
2 teaspoons kirsch
1 cup heavy cream
1 pound nectarines, peeled and stoned
¼ cup corn syrup (optional)

1. Boil sugar and water together for 5 minutes; cool. In the blender, process together the eggs, lemon juice, and kirsch.
2. With the motor running, slowly pour the cream into the blender, and finally add pieces of nectarine. Blend to a smooth puree. Taste for sweetness. Add a little corn syrup, if needed.
3. Pour the mixture into an ice cream maker and freeze. If you don't have an ice cream maker, pour mixture into a 9-inch round cake pan and place in the freezer; when the mixture is a little mushy, beat with a wire whisk to break down the ice

crystals, and then refreeze. When refreezing, the ice cream can be put in a decorative mold or soufflé dish.

PINEAPPLE UPSIDE-DOWN CAKE WITH RUM

Don't worry about serving your guests rum at lunch. Once the golden liquor reaches the boiling point, all the alcohol has burned off. This is an especially cheery dessert for a dreary February day.

Makes 1 9- or 10-inch cake

8 tablespoons butter (1 stick)
1 cup brown sugar, firmly packed
8 slices unsweetened pineapple
4 eggs, separated
1 tablespoon melted butter
1 teaspoon vanilla extract
½ teaspoon nutmeg
pinch of salt
1 cup sugar, sifted
1 cup cake flour
1 teaspoon baking powder
1½ cups pineapple juice
¼ cup dark rum

Preheat oven to 350 degrees.

1. Select a 9- or 10-inch iron skillet or cake pan; a heat-deflector pad will be necessary if you use a cake pan. Melt the stick of butter in the skillet or cake pan. Stir in the brown sugar and cook over low heat until the sugar is completely dissolved. Arrange the pineapple slices in the melted sugar in a symmetrical pattern (this will be the top of the finished cake).

2. In a mixing bowl, beat the egg yolks until thick and pale yellow, then add 1 tablespoon melted butter, vanilla, and nutmeg. In a separate bowl beat the egg whites with a pinch of salt. When the whites begin to hold their shape, slowly add the

sifted sugar. Fold the stiffly beaten whites into the yolk mixture.

3. Sift the flour and baking powder together and fold them into the batter gently about 1/4 cup at a time. Spoon the batter over the pineapple-sugar layer, smoothing the top neatly. Bake for about 25 to 30 minutes or until the cake puffs a little and turns golden.

4. Remove the cake from the oven and let cool for 15 minutes. If serving immediately, turn it out upside down on a serving dish. If the cake has been baked in advance, leave it in the skillet or cake pan and when ready to serve, warm in a 325-degree oven for about 10 minutes.

5. Boil the pineapple juice until it reduces to 1 cup. (This can be done in advance.) Just before serving, reheat the juice and add the rum; bring to a boil. Pour the juice into a sauceboat and serve at once to be poured over the warm cake.

The Tea Party

In many countries, tea or coffee is the focal point of a late-afternoon ritual. The four- or five-o'clock high tea in England is, to all intents and purposes, a small meal that can replace the evening repast, if one so chooses. Le Goûter in France is a delicious bite, usually sweet, to enjoy with afternoon tea, coffee, or hot chocolate. Viennese pastries are devoured around the clock, but never with more relish than when they are an unnecessary indulgence that accompany coffee mit schlag as you watch the light begin to fade. Decades ago the tea dance was American high society's way of passing the waning hours of the afternoon, and recently there has been a revival of that charming musical hour.

These are all small celebrations with an air of informality. The tea party can fit effortlessly and inexpensively into an entertaining scheme at home. There are no hard-and-fast rules for what to serve, other than tea and/or coffee, of course. The table can hold fresh cut-up fruit (a thoughtful addition among the calorie blockbusters), sweets like fruitcake cut into small fingers of lusciousness, hot crêpes with fresh fruit or sauce (for this you need serving help), and even cold strawberry soup served in punch glasses.

The afternoon tea party is one of the easiest for an inexperienced hostess to bring off. The refreshments can be ordered from a caterer or a shop if time or baking ability are lacking. *None of the food served is expensive, so even if it's bought ready-made, the overall cost of the party will not be burdensome.*

The tea table must be large enough to accommodate a tea service at one end and coffee at the other. Several smaller tables can be used, instead. Cover the table or tables with your prettiest cloths. Arrange cups and tea-spoons on saucers around both pouring stations so that they are readily available to the hostess. Brew a strong tea extract that can be diluted to any desired strength with hot water and provide both cold milk and lemon. The food, small plates, folded napkins, and forks should be placed in the center of the table within easy reach.

Depending on the size and formality of the party, you may have your friends pour tea themselves or, more correctly, ask one or two guests to serve as hostesses and pour. For large parties, it is necessary to have one woman pouring tea while another pours coffee. A thoughtful hostess will ask others to replace them after about 20 minutes.

The recipes that follow offer a diversity of flavors and richness. The section opens with Paskha, *a smooth Russian cheese dessert, and includes a cold fruit omelet, cookies, cakes, and yeast pastries. It comes to a close with a flourish with heady Irish coffee—a brew not often considered for this amiable time of the day.*

PASKHA (RUSSIAN EASTER DESSERT)

Paskha, a wonderfully rich cheese dessert, is the centerpiece of Russian Easter tables. Traditionally pyramid-shaped, it is decorated with the letters XB, the abbreviation for *Christos Voskres* (Christ is Risen) in the Cyrillic alphabet. *Paskha* is also the Russian word for Easter. I have always felt that this luscious cake should be enjoyed year-round, with or without the decoration. A small slice at teatime outshines most other pastries. This version is different from and easier than many; nonetheless, it is authentic—I learned it from a wonderful White Russian countess in Paris.

Serves 8 to 10

3 pounds cottage cheese
¼ pound butter
¾ cup sugar
1 teaspoon salt
¾ cup sour cream
2 egg yolks
¼ cup almonds (toasted and ground fine)
1½ teaspoons vanilla
2 teaspoons grated lemon rind
½ cup seedless raisins
½ cup candied fruits (optional)

1. Drain the cottage cheese in a colander for at least 1 hour; press from time to time to squeeze out as much liquid as possible. Push the drained cottage cheese through a fine sieve or puree attachment on an electric mixer. Work the butter through the sieve or puree attachment and mix with cottage cheese. Beat the mixture with an electric beater until it is very smooth.

2. Sift in the sugar and salt. Beat in the sour cream, egg yolks, and ground almonds, then add the vanilla and lemon

rind. Beat until very smooth. Finally, fold in the raisins and candied fruit, if desired.

3. Select a 6-cup mold with a drain hole in the bottom. (If you lack the traditional mold, try using a new flowerpot, a colander, or a 2-pound coffee can or plastic container with holes poked in the cover. The only requirement is the drain hole.) Line the mold with cheesecloth, allowing at least 4 inches of fabric to lap over the edge (this overlap helps in removing the dessert later). Spoon the mixture into the mold, pressing down to fill all cracks and holes. Tap the mold sharply on the counter to settle the mixture well into the bottom. Smooth the top and fold the extra cheesecloth over it.

4. Place the mold over a deep bowl or pot that is a little smaller than the mold, allowing the suspended mold to drip into the bowl. Put a heavy weight on top of the mixture, and place in the refrigerator for 2 days. From time to time discard the liquid that collects in the bowl. As the liquid is forced from the *Paskha* it will become firm.

5. To remove the *Paskha,* tap the mold sharply a few times on the countertop, then tug gently at the loose edges of the cheesecloth until the dessert is loosened. Invert the *Paskha* onto a serving dish and use a spatula or wide knife to smooth out the cheesecloth markings.

NOTE: To decorate the *Paskha* use angelica, candied fruit, or raisins to form the initials XB on two sides, and create whatever shapes you fancy on the other sides. Place a small birthday candle on top and a few jelly beans around the dish. Cut slices horizontally across the *Paskha.* It is very rich, so cut thin slices.

COLD PEACH OMELET

I can't decide whether I prefer this dessert omelet at room temperature or well chilled. The flavor is ethereally delicate when it's still vaguely warm. On the other hand, leaving it for a few hours in the refrigerator tends to intensify the taste of the peaches. Take your pick.

Serves 8

2½ tablespoons butter
¾ pound (about 3 or 4) peaches, freshly sliced
1½ tablespoons brown sugar
5 eggs, separated
1¼ cups heavy cream
3 tablespoons flour
2 teaspoons orange liqueur
1 teaspoon vanilla extract
pinch of cream of tartar
sugar

Preheat oven to 425 degrees.

1. Grease an 8- or 9-inch pie dish with ½ tablespoon of the butter and set aside. Melt the remaining 2 tablespoons of butter in a nonreactive skillet (enameled, stainless-steel, copper, or fine cast aluminum) and add the sliced peaches. Sprinkle 1 tablespoon of the brown sugar over peaches, stir with a wooden spoon, cover, and simmer gently for 2 minutes. Remove at once from the heat, and set aside six of the best-looking slices to use as a garnish.

2. In the jar of a blender, combine the egg yolks, ¼ cup of the cream, the flour, orange liqueur, and vanilla. Blend thoroughly. Scrape the peaches and melted butter into the blender and puree.

3. Add the cream of tartar to the egg whites and beat until firm. Carefully pour the batter from the blender down the side of the egg-white bowl; do not pour into the center of the beaten whites. Delicately fold the batter into the whites. Do not overmix. Pour the omelet batter into the prepared pie dish and smooth the top with a rubber spatula. Arrange the reserved peach slices in a circle near the center of the dish and sprinkle the top with the remaining ½ tablespoon brown sugar. Bake for

15 minutes or until the omelet is nicely puffed and brown in spots.

4. Serve at room temperature or well chilled. Whip the remaining cup of cream and flavor it with a little sugar and additional orange liqueur if desired. Pass with the omelet.

RASPBERRY BUTTONS

Although these red-topped, tasty morsels are especially attractive on trays of holiday cookies, they are appreciated at any time of year. They keep very well in a loosely covered container. For variety, fill the cookies with other jams or even with chocolate.

Makes about 5 dozen

> 1 cup shortening
> ½ cup brown sugar
> 2 eggs, separated
> ¼ teaspoon salt
> 2 to 2½ cups sifted flour
> 2 cups chopped nuts or coconut
> ½ cup raspberry jam

1. Cream together the shortening, sugar, egg yolks, salt, and enough flour to make a stiff dough that will not stick to the hands. Chill for at least 30 minutes.

Preheat oven to 375 degrees.

2. Grease a cookie sheet. Roll bits of the chilled dough into 1-inch balls. Holding a cookie ball on the end of a fork, dip it into a saucer containing the egg whites, then drop it into a saucer containing the nuts or coconut. Roll the cookie around in the nuts or coconut to coat it evenly. Repeat until all of the balls are coated.

3. Place the cookies about 1 inch apart on the cookie sheet. Make a slight depression on the top of each cookie. (A thimble dipped in flour works well.) Bake the cookies for 5 minutes.

4. Press the centers again and fill them with raspberry jam. Return the cookies to the oven for about 7 or 8 minutes or until they turn a pale golden color.

SOUR CREAM CRISSCROSSES

This recipe used to be filed under "Cookies," but now I tend to think of these tidbits as a pastry or small cake. They are rich and addictively delicious. The sour cream dough may prove difficult to roll for the crisscross strips on top; if so, use a floured rolling pin and roll out the dough on a cookie sheet to an 8 × 6-inch rectangle, freeze for 10 minutes, then cut into strips. If the dough becomes soft while you're working with it, return it to the freezer to firm.

Makes about 4¹/₂ dozen cookies

1 cup butter, softened
1½ cups sugar
3 eggs
1 cup sour cream
3½ cups flour
1 tablespoon baking powder
½ teaspoon salt
2 cups strawberry preserves
¼ pound walnuts, ground

1. Cream the butter and sugar together well; add 1 whole egg and 2 yolks, reserving the 2 whites. Beat in the sour cream.
2. Combine 3 cups of flour, baking powder, and salt in a sifter and gradually sift into the creamed mixture, stirring well after each addition.
3. Select a jelly roll pan about 13 × 18 × 1 inches and spoon about two-thirds of the dough into the pan. Using a long-bladed spatula or your hands, spread or pat the dough into an even layer about ¼ inch thick. Spread the preserves over the

dough and sprinkle with half the ground nuts. Let stand at room temperature.

4. Stir the remaining ½ cup of flour into the remaining one-third of dough. Cover tightly and chill at least 1 hour. Then roll out half the remaining dough into an 8 × 6-inch rectangle, keeping the other half refrigerated, and cut into ¼-inch-wide strips. Lay parallel strips diagonally over the preserves, leaving about 1½ inches between the strips. Brush with reserved egg whites, slightly beaten. Preheat oven to 350 degrees.

5. Roll out the refrigerated dough, arrange another layer of strips in crisscross fashion, and brush with egg whites. Sprinkle on remaining nuts. Bake for 30 to 35 minutes or until the dough has turned a deep golden color. Cool, then cut into squares.

PURE STRAWBERRY PIE

Unlike most fruit tarts, there is no custard cream under the strawberries in this recipe; it is replaced by a strawberry custard that is spooned over fresh strawberries. This is strawberries all the way, and doubly good for it.

Serves 8

1 9-inch pastry shell, baked (pages 247–48)
3 pints fresh strawberries
⅓ cup cornstarch
1 cup sugar
2 tablespoons lemon juice
1 teaspoon orange liqueur
1 cup heavy cream, whipped and sweetened

1. Wash, hull, and dry the strawberries. Reserve about 2 cups of the largest and best-looking berries.

2. In a heavy pot, mash the remaining 4 cups of berries. Add the cornstarch, sugar, and lemon juice and stir well. Cook the

mixture over low to moderate heat, stirring constantly, until it becomes thick and turns clear. Add the orange liqueur and cook 1 minute longer. Cool, then chill.

3. At serving time, set aside a few whole berries from the reserved 2 cups. Cut the rest of the remaining berries in half lengthwise and place them in the bottom of the baked pie shell, cut-side down.

4. Spoon the chilled strawberry custard over the berries and smooth the top nicely. Spread the whipped cream over the top of the pie, leaving a large circle in the center exposed to contrast the red custard with the white cream. Decorate the pie by placing the few reserved whole berries in the center.

NOTE: If the pie must be assembled ahead of time, try to limit its standing time to 2 or 3 hours because the juice of the fresh berries will cause the crust to become a little limp.

TARTE AUX POMMES FRANGIPANE (APPLE TART WITH ALMOND PASTE)

This may not be a very deep pie, but what is there is delicious. A toothsome almond paste provides a rich counterpoint to the not-too-sweet apples, and a film of shiny apricot glaze completes the picture. For teatime, cut the tart into thin wedges.

Makes 1 10-inch tart

1 cup blanched whole almonds
¾ cup sugar
¼ teaspoon grated nutmeg
1 egg
4 tablespoons unsalted butter
Pastry (pages 247–48)
1 pound Golden Delicious apples
6 tablespoons apricot jelly (not jam)
3 tablespoons water
2 teaspoons kirsch (optional)

1. Put the almonds in the bowl of a blender or food processor. Operate the machine in short bursts to reduce the nuts to a fine powder. Add ½ cup sugar, nutmeg, egg, and 2 tablespoons melted butter and blend to make a smooth paste.
Preheat oven to 400 degrees.
2. Roll out the pastry and place in a 10-inch pie pan. Spread the almond filling smoothly over the pastry.
3. Peel, halve, and core the apples, and cut into slices about ¼ inch thick. Arrange the apple slices in an overlapping pattern of concentric circles to fill the entire pan. Sprinkle on 2 tablespoons of sugar and dot with 2 tablespoons of butter.
4. Bake the tart for about 45 minutes or until the apples are tender and the pastry has browned nicely. Cool.
5. Combine the apricot jelly with 2 tablespoons of sugar and three tablespoons of water in a small saucepan. Bring to a boil and simmer for about 5 minutes. Cool and add the kirsch, if desired. Brush the glaze over the cold pie and allow to set for about 15 minutes.

TARTE AUX POMMES NORMANDE (APPLE AND CREAM TART)

When a French dish is called *Normande* it will probably contain either apples or cream and usually both, since these are two principal products of Normandy. If you find that not all the cream sauce will fit in the tart, add some cinnamon and freshly grated nutmeg to the leftover cream and pour it into small custard cups. Place the cups in a small pan partly filled with water and bake until set, and you will have a delicious custard as a bonus for making the tart.

Makes 1 deep 10-inch tart

Pastry (pages 247–48)
1 pound apples (York, Stayman, or Roman)
3 tablespoons flour
½ cup sugar

2 eggs
3 egg yolks
2 cups light cream
2 teaspoons vanilla
powdered sugar

Preheat oven to 375 degrees.

1. Line a 10-inch pie pan with pastry. Peel, halve, and core the apples, then cut into slices about ¼ inch thick. Pile the apples in the pastry-lined pie pan, taking care to smooth the top.

2. Mix the flour and sugar in a bowl; make a well in the center and add the eggs and egg yolks. With a wire whisk beat the eggs, then incorporate the dry ingredients into them. Slowly pour in the cream while continuing to whisk; finally stir in the vanilla. Carefully pour this cream sauce over the apples.

3. Bake the tart for about 1 hour or until the custard has set. Test by inserting a small sharp knife into the custard; it should come out clean and almost dry. Remove tart from the oven and cool. Just before serving, sprinkle with powdered sugar.

BLUEBERRY PIE

Just hearing the words "blueberry cake" or "blueberry pie" can excite my taste buds. This all-American berry varies in sweetness during its summer growing season and may be quite tart; the amount of sugar added should be adjusted accordingly. Frozen unsweetened berries can be used when the fresh have disappeared, but measure them *before* defrosting. Once defrosted they collapse and give a compacted, false measure.

Makes 1 9-inch pie

1 prebaked 9-inch pie shell (pages 247–48)
2 cups blueberries
2⅓ cups water
¼ to ½ cup sugar
¼ teaspoon nutmeg
½ teaspoon grated orange rind
2 tablespoons cornstarch
1 tablespoon kirsch
1 tablespoon lemon juice
1 tablespoon gelatin
½ cup heavy cream

1. Pick the stems off the berries and rinse. Put the berries in a saucepan and add 2 cups of water, ¼ cup of sugar, nutmeg, and orange rind. In a small bowl mix the cornstarch, kirsch, 2 tablespoons of water, and lemon juice into a paste. Add this paste to the blueberries. Place the pan over medium heat and slowly bring to the boiling point; simmer for 5 minutes while stirring. The opaque sauce should become thick and translucent.

2. While the berries are cooking, soften the gelatin in the remaining 3 tablespoons of water. As soon as the pan of berries is taken off the heat, add the gelatin and stir until it is completely dissolved. Taste for sweetness and add extra sugar, if necessary.

3. Cool the filling, then chill until it begins to set. Spoon the filling into the pie shell, smooth the top, and refrigerate to set the gelatin. Just before serving, whip the cream until stiff, flavoring with a little sugar and kirsch or orange liqueur. Cover the pie evenly with the whipped cream.

POPPYSEED PIE

Poppyseed is so little used in American kitchens that it is sold by spice companies in small jars. Larger, more economical amounts can be found at ethnic and health-food stores; the tiny seeds tend to be fresher when bought there, too. Here is one unusual way to use them.

Makes 1 9-inch pie

Pastry for 1 9-inch pie (pages 247–48)
2½ cups milk
⅔ cup poppyseed
6 tablespoons sugar
½ cup semolina or farina
½ cup cream
1 egg, lightly beaten
2 teaspoons vanilla
½ teaspoon grated orange rind

Topping:
1 egg
2 tablespoons sugar
1 tablespoon flour
1 cup sour cream
1 teaspoon vanilla

Preheat oven to 350 degrees.
1. Line a 9-inch pie pan with the pastry. While bringing ½ cup milk to a boil, measure the poppyseed and sugar into a medium-size mixing bowl. Pour the hot milk over the poppy-

seed, stir quickly to dissolve the sugar, cover, and put aside for 15 minutes.

2. Heat 2 more cups of milk to the simmering point. Slowly stir in the semolina or farina, lower the heat, and cook for about 3 minutes or until quite thick. Cool for 5 minutes, then beat the semolina into the poppyseed mixture. Beat together the cream, egg, and vanilla and then add to the poppyseed mixture. Stir well to completely blend all the ingredients, add the orange rind, and stir again. Scoop the poppyseed filling into the pastry-lined pie pan and smooth the top.

3. In a small bowl beat together all the ingredients for the topping. Spoon this flavored cream over the poppyseed. Bake for 30 to 35 minutes or until a knife plunged in the center comes out clean. The topping may puff in some spots during the baking; once out of the oven it will collapse into an even coating.

WALNUT CHIFFON PIE

This is a rich pie with a luxuriously velvety texture and should be served in small wedges. So unless you are entertaining a large group, you might prefer to make an 8-inch pie with only half the amount of filling.

Makes 1 12-inch pie

1 baked 12-inch pie shell (pages 247–48)
¼ cup water
1 tablespoon gelatin
¾ cup milk
⅛ teaspoon cinnamon
¼ cup brown sugar
2 tablespoons honey
3 eggs, separated
1 cup ground walnuts
¼ teaspoon maple extract
1 tablespoon vanilla

pinch of cream of tartar
¾ cup heavy cream
Garnish: 10 walnut halves
         1 egg white
         sugar

1. Pour the water into a small cup, sprinkle the gelatin over it, and put aside to soften. Pour the milk into a heavy saucepan, add the cinnamon, sugar, and honey, and bring to the boiling point. Beat the egg yolks in a bowl. Slowly pour into them about half the hot flavored milk, whisking vigorously all the time. Return the egg yolk-milk mixture to the pot and, stirring constantly, cook until the custard thickens enough to coat a spoon. Stir in the softened gelatin and mix until it dissolves. Add the walnuts and maple extract and cook for 1 minute more. Scrape the custard back into the mixing bowl, stir for a few minutes to cool, then add the vanilla. Put aside for about 1 hour to cool and thicken: the thickening can be hastened by chilling the mixture in the refrigerator after it has cooled.

2. Beat the egg whites until quite firm, adding a little cream of tartar if not using a copper bowl. Fold about a third of the beaten whites into the thickened nut custard and incorporate thoroughly with the whisk. Give the beaten whites a few more whisks, scrape them over the filling and lightly fold them in with a rubber spatula. Refrigerate for 30 minutes. Beat the cream until very stiff and fold into the chilled nut filling. Immediately scoop the filling into the prepared pie shell, smooth the top and refrigerate.

3. To prepare the walnut garnish, preheat the oven to 350 degrees. Lightly beat the egg white with a fork. Place a walnut half on the fork and dip it into the white, then transfer the egg-coated walnut to a baking sheet by pushing it off the fork with another fork. Dip 6 of the walnut halves this way and sprinkle a little sugar over them. Bake the nuts for about 5 minutes or until the coating has lightly browned. Remove at once from the baking sheet. Decorate the pie just before serving by alternating 4 of the coated nuts with 4 of the plain nut halves in a circular shape; place 2 coated nuts in the center in a V shape.

about 30 minutes or until the center is slightly puffed and the sides begin to pull away from the pan. Cool. Sprinkle with powdered sugar.

ANGEL FOOD CAKE

The array of temptations put before guests at teatime should include several things dieters can be comfortable with. Sliced fresh fruit and berries are always appreciated, but something as wicked-looking as Angel Food Cake also fits the bill. There is not a trace of fat of any kind in Angel Food Cake, and it's fat that carries a calorie wallop. Even the sugar has been trimmed way down in this recipe, so that each slice is a mere 107 calories. Serve plain with sliced strawberries on the side.

Serves 12

1 cup sifted cake flour
½ teaspoon salt
1 cup sugar
1¼ cups egg whites (about 10 eggs), at room temperature
1 teaspoon cream of tartar
1 tablespoon warm water
1 tablespoon lemon juice, at room temperature
1 teaspoon vanilla
½ teaspoon almond extract

Preheat oven to 350 degrees.
1. Combine the sifted flour with the salt and ¼ cup of sugar and resift 4 times, holding the sifter high above the bowl to incorporate as much air as possible. Sift the remaining ¾ cup sugar into another bowl.
2. Start beating the egg whites and, when they are foamy, add the cream of tartar. Beat for half a minute longer, then add the water and lemon juice and beat until the whites are stiff but not dry.
3. Begin adding the sifted sugar a tablespoon at a time while

continuing to beat. Each addition must be thoroughly dissolved before more sugar is put in. After all the sugar has been incorporated, beat in the vanilla and almond extract.

4. Sift about a quarter of the flour-and-sugar mixture over the beaten whites, then fold in lightly and carefully with a rubber spatula. Continue gradually sifting and folding in until all the remaining dry ingredients have been worked in.

5. Carefully spoon the batter into an ungreased 9- or 10-inch tube pan. Smooth the surface lightly with a rubber spatula. With a stainless steel or silver knife, cut through the batter in a circle to eliminate any air pockets. Bake for 40 to 45 minutes or until the top is a dark golden color and the cake springs back when pressed. Remove from the oven and cool upside down. (Some angel food pans have feet on them for this purpose, thus raising the pan enough to allow air to circulate around the cake. If you lack such a pan, invert the tube onto a bottle, funnel, or glass, or place on a cake rack.) Allow the cake to cool for about 2 hours.

6. To remove the cake from the pan, use a sharp, thin knife to cut around the outside edge and the center tube. Push the detachable bottom upward and lift the cake away. Carefully cut the cake loose from the metal bottom.

7. Do not use a knife to cut the cake; instead, pull slices apart with two large forks. If you can find an angel food cake fork, so much the better, but they seem to have disappeared from the market.

VARIATION: Angel Food Cupcakes with Raspberry Sauce
Use the same batter as for the preceding Angel Food Cake, but bake it in muffin pans. Calories are cut down even more, since the cupcakes are smaller than tall slices. There will be about 16 cupcakes. Serve with Raspberry Sauce (page 250).

LINZER TORTE

I strongly recommend making your own applesauce for this exceptional pastry. Canned applesauce tends to be quite sweet, but you can temper the amount of sugar to allow for the sweetness of the raspberry jam.

Makes 1 9-inch tart

Pastry:
2½ cups flour
2 teaspoons cinnamon
½ cup powdered almonds
½ cup sugar
pinch salt
8 tablespoons unsalted butter
2 teaspoons vanilla
½ cup cold water

Filling:
1 cup applesauce
1½ cups raspberry jam (not jelly)
½ teaspoon cinnamon
½ teaspoon nutmeg
1 teaspoon vanilla
1 teaspoon kirsch (or other fruit liqueur)

1. To make pastry, mix the flour, cinnamon, powdered almonds, sugar, and salt. Cut in the butter with a pastry blender or two knives. Add the vanilla and just enough cold water to make the mixture form a ball. Knead for 1 minute, seal in a plastic bag, and refrigerate for at least 1 hour.

Preheat oven to 350 degrees.

2. Either roll out enough dough to fit a 9-inch pie pan or pat it into pan with floured fingertips. It should be about ¼ inch thick. Keep the rest of the dough chilled. Spoon in the applesauce and smooth it into a layer. Thoroughly blend together

the remaining filling ingredients, then spoon over the apple-sauce.

3. Roll out the rest of the dough and cut in strips with a pastry cutter. Arrange the strips in a lattice pattern on top of the tart. Bake for 5 minutes, then reduce the oven temperature to 325 degrees and bake 40 to 45 minutes more or until the pastry is a deep golden color.

MAPLE CAKE MARVEL

What's so marvelous about this cake? The fact that it is both delicious and easy to prepare, that's what. Better still, the cake is mixed right in its baking pan, which means no bowl to wash.

Makes 1 9-inch single-layer cake

2 cups flour
¼ cup sugar
½ teaspoon salt
2 teaspoons baking soda
1 tablespoon vanilla
¾ cup pure maple syrup
½ cup water
2 teaspoons imitation maple flavoring
2 tablespoons rum
1 cup oil
3 tablespoons vinegar (not wine vinegar)
powdered sugar

Preheat oven to 375 degrees.

1. Measure into a 9-inch cake pan the flour, sugar, salt, and baking soda; stir to blend the dry ingredients. Add the vanilla, maple syrup, water, maple flavoring, rum, and oil and stir with a fork or wire whisk until all ingredients are thoroughly blended.

2. Add the vinegar and mix again to distribute it throughout the cake. Immediately place cake in the oven and bake for

APPLE COFFEE CAKE

This excellent coffee-cake loaf can be enriched by the addition of walnuts or pecans. The cake is best, of course, when fresh, but it also refrigerates and freezes very well. This is a handy loaf to have waiting in the freezer for sudden needs.

Makes 1 8 x 4-inch loaf

½ pound (2 or 3) tart apples
8 tablespoons butter
2 eggs
1 cup sugar
2 tablespoons buttermilk
1 teaspoon vanilla extract
½ teaspoon cinnamon
¼ teaspoon nutmeg
¼ teaspoon salt
2 teaspoons baking powder
½ teaspoon baking soda
2 cups flour

Preheat oven to 350 degrees.

1. Peel, quarter, core, and grate the apples. In a heavy skillet, melt the butter. Add the apples, turning them over and over to thoroughly coat the fruit with the butter. Simmer for 30 seconds and remove from heat at once. Set aside.

2. Beat together the eggs and sugar, then add the milk, vanilla, cinnamon, nutmeg, salt, baking powder, and baking soda. Mix very well. Add the flour slowly and beat in thoroughly. Fold in the apples and melted butter.

3. Grease and flour an 8¼ x 4½ x 2½-inch loaf pan and pour in the batter. Bake for 50 to 55 minutes or until the top surface cracks and a toothpick plunged in the center comes out clean. Remove from the pan while still slightly warm.

EASY COFFEE CAKE

This is not a coffee-flavored cake, but the sort of good, well-made cake that seems to demand a steaming cup of tea or coffee to accompany it. Quality is not always measured by complexity, as this simple cake proves.

Makes 1 8 x 10-inch cake

1½ cups flour
1 cup sugar
2 teaspoons baking powder
½ teaspoon salt
1 cup sour cream
½ teaspoon baking soda
2 eggs
1 tablespoon butter
Topping: 1 tablespoon sugar
2 teaspoons cinnamon
⅛ teaspoon nutmeg

Preheat oven to 350 degrees.

1. Sift together the flour, sugar, baking powder, and salt. In a small bowl, beat together the sour cream, baking soda, and eggs; then stir mixture into the dry ingredients. Beat the batter well.

2. Spread the batter into a greased 8 x 10-inch baking pan and bake for about 35 minutes or until a toothpick plunged in the center comes out dry.

3. While the cake is baking, mix together the tablespoon of sugar, cinnamon, and nutmeg. Immediately upon removing the cake from the oven, rub the butter over the hot surface and sprinkle with the flavored sugar. Cool.

CHERRY COBBLER

In America, cobblers are as traditional as apple pie, but one encounters them much less frequently. Perhaps they are overlooked because cobblers are not showy-looking. Well, neither is caviar, which in no way diminishes its worth.

Serves 10 to 12

8 tablespoons butter, cut into pieces
1 cup flour
1 cup sugar
3 teaspoons baking powder
¼ teaspoon salt
1 cup milk
½ teaspoon vanilla
2 pounds fresh cherries, pitted
1 pint heavy cream (optional)

Preheat oven to 375 degrees.

1. Place the butter in a 9 x 13-inch pan or ovenproof dish and put in the oven until the butter melts. Carefully remove the pan and tilt it so that the butter completely covers the bottom.

2. Measure the flour, sugar, baking powder, and salt into a bowl. Stir the milk in slowly to keep the mixture smooth, then add the vanilla. Pour the batter into the pan directly over the butter and spread into an even layer.

3. Scatter the cherries over the top of the batter. Bake cobbler for 40 to 45 minutes or until the top is a deep golden brown.

NOTE: It is best to serve the cobbler while it's still warm, since its puffiness disappears as the cake cools. If you serve it cold, whip the optional cream and sweeten it with sugar, then cover the cobbler with the whipped cream.

PETER'S TORTE CAKE

Every cook needs at least one quick-and-sure cake recipe. This rich and handsome striped cake takes less than 10 minutes to put together, and few guests would suspect that it wasn't made from scratch. Does it matter when it tastes so good?

Serves 16

1 ready-made pound cake
1 teaspoon instant coffee
1 tablespoon boiling water
6-ounce package chocolate chips
1 cup sour cream

1. Freeze the cake for about 20 minutes to firm it, making slicing easier. Cut the cake horizontally with a long, sharp knife to produce seven layers with the bottom layer a little thicker than the rest. (Seven layers is ideal, but fewer layers still makes a very good cake.)

2. Dissolve the instant coffee in the boiling water in the top of a double boiler suspended over, not in, simmering water. Add the chocolate chips and melt them, stirring often. When the chocolate is completely smooth, remove the pan from the heat, cool for 2 minutes, then stir in the sour cream.

3. Generously frost each layer of cake with the chocolate icing, restacking the layers, then cover the entire cake with the icing. Refrigerate for at least 2 days. (The cake will keep for several weeks in the refrigerator.) It is very rich, so slice razor thin.

BABA AU RHUM

These sweet, leavened cakes have some of the characteristics of *brioche*. The *baba* is said to have been made famous by King Stanislaus of Poland, who was so fond of them that he had them prepared for his state visit to France in the early seventeenth century.

Makes 12 Babas

Babas:
1½ cups white flour
1 package active dry yeast
2 tablespoons tepid water
1 teaspoon salt
2 tablespoons sugar
2 large eggs
4 tablespoons butter, melted and cooled

Rum Syrup:
2 cups water
1 cup sugar
½ cup dark rum

Apricot Glaze:
3 tablespoons apricot jam
2 teaspoons water (approximately)

1. Put the flour in a deep mixing bowl, make a well in the center, and put the yeast in the well. Add the tepid water and let it stand for a few seconds to dissolve the yeast. Add the salt, sugar, and eggs to the well. Using the tips of the fingers, blend together the ingredients in the center, then gradually incorporate the flour. When all the ingredients have been worked together, knead for at least 5 minutes.
2. Add the cooled, melted butter and knead again to incor-

porate it. Place the dough in a greased bowl, cover, and let stand in a warm place for 1½ to 2 hours or until the dough has doubled in bulk. Test by pressing your finger in the center of the dough; the depression should remain.

Preheat oven to 375 degrees.

3. Butter 12 *baba* molds, custard cups, or a 12-cup muffin tin. Deflate the dough by kneading gently with your fingertips. Break off enough dough to fill each mold one-third full and press the dough lightly into the bottom of the mold. Place the uncovered molds in a warm place and let the dough rise again until it expands ¼ inch above the tops of the molds. Bake at once for about 15 minutes or until the *babas* are nicely browned and have shrunk slightly away from the sides of the molds.

4. While the *babas* are baking, make the rum syrup. Boil 2 cups of water and the sugar together for 2 minutes; remove from the heat and stir in the rum.

5. Before the *babas* have cooled completely, prick the tops and sides of the warm cakes and place them in a deep dish. Pour the lukewarm rum syrup over them and let stand for 30 minutes, basting occasionally. (A bulb baster works well for this.) Drain on a rack.

6. While the *babas* are soaking, make the apricot glaze. Force the apricot jam through a strainer into a small pan, add approximately 2 teaspoons of water, just enough to start the jam melting, and place over medium heat. Mix with a wire whisk until the jam has melted. Brush this glaze over the tops of the drained *babas*.

NOTE: *Babas* are best eaten the day they are prepared, but will keep in the refrigerator for a day or two.

KOLACHE (COLD DOUGH YEAST COOKIES)

No middle European holiday, wedding, or special dinner would be considered complete without crisp, flaky, and tenderly flavorful *Kolache*. If a variety of fillings are used, you have a perfect excuse to try another and still another.

Makes 5 to 6 dozen

½ pound (1 cup) vegetable shortening
½ pound butter
5 eggs, beaten
⅔-ounce cake compressed yeast or 2 teaspoons dry yeast
1 cup lukewarm milk
1 teaspoon vanilla extract
5 to 6 cups flour
2 teaspoons baking powder
1 teaspoon salt
confectioners' sugar
Fillings: stewed apricots, poppyseed filling, prune butter, almond paste, or ground walnuts moistened with warm milk and a little vanilla and sugar.

1. Cream the shortening and butter together until very soft. Add the beaten eggs and blend well.
2. Dissolve the yeast in the lukewarm milk, then add to the egg mixture. Stir in the vanilla.
3. Sift together 4 cups of the flour, the baking powder, and salt and stir into the shortening mixture. Knead the dough, adding the remaining flour a little at a time until the dough no longer sticks to your hands. Cover tightly and refrigerate overnight.
Preheat oven to 350 degrees.
4. Take a large handful of the dough and roll it in confectioners' sugar. On a lightly floured board, roll the dough into a large square or rectangle about ¼ inch thick. Cut the dough into 2- to 3-inch squares.
5. Place a teaspoon of filling in the center of each square. Form the squares into little packages, pinching two opposite corners of each square over the filling, or pinwheels, slashing each square diagonally through the corners and then lifting every other halved corner and pinching the four pieces of dough together in the center to form the top of the cookie.

6. Place the cookies 3 inches apart on an ungreased baking sheet. Bake for 20 to 25 minutes or until golden brown. When the cookies have cooled a little, sprinkle with sifted confectioners' sugar to give a shiny coating.

BLACK CHOCOLATE CAKE

I started to title this sinfully rich cake Flourless Chocolate Cake, then realized that the reader would probably consider it a diet cake and pass right over it. Believe me, it is anything but. Flour is eliminated so that the chocolate flavor will not be attenuated. This fudgelike cake is deep in flavor and dense in texture and I suggest serving it in small wedges. It should be made several days in advance and refrigerated.

Serves 8 to 10

½ cup strong coffee
7 ounces bittersweet chocolate, broken into pieces
8 ounces unsalted butter, cut into pieces
1 cup sugar
4 eggs
1 teaspoon rum
Crème Anglaise (Light Custard Sauce) (pages 249–50) or
  vanilla ice cream

Preheat oven to 350 degrees.
1. Select an 8-inch springform pan that does not leak and generously butter and flour it. If the pan leaks a little, wrap aluminum foil around the bottom half. The leaking will stop after several minutes in the oven.
2. Pour the coffee into a heavy saucepan and, stirring often, melt the chocolate in it over medium heat. Reduce the heat to low, add about a fifth each of the butter and sugar, and stir until the butter melts and the sugar dissolves. Continue adding the butter and sugar a little at a time, blending them very well into the chocolate before any further additions. Remove the pan

from the heat and let cool for 5 minutes. Beat the eggs and the rum together, then whisk them into the chocolate batter until thoroughly blended. Work quickly to prevent the eggs from starting to cook in the hot batter.

3. Pour the batter into the prepared cake pan. Bake for about 45 minutes or until a thin crust has formed on top and the sides of the cake begin to pull away from the pan. Since the cake bakes much as a soufflé—from the outside in—the center will be slightly concave until it too is baked through and then the top levels out. The cake will rise a little during the baking, then collapse into a layer about 1 ½ inches thick.

4. Cool the cake. Remove the band of the springform pan, but leave the cake resting on the pan bottom. Cover and refrigerate for 1 to 3 days. Remove the cake from the refrigerator about 2 hours before serving and transfer the cake from the pan bottom to a serving dish. Take the custard sauce out 30 minutes before serving dessert.

IRISH COFFEE

Why Irish Coffee at teatime? Why not? It's a drink almost everyone warms to, but it usually is timidly reserved for Saint Patrick's Day or after dinner. I wouldn't suggest it for a working tea or coffee hour, but it is a cheery addition just about any other time.

Serves 6

> 6 to 12 teaspoons sugar
> 6 ounces Irish whiskey (traditionally) or Scotch whiskey
>   (untraditionally)
> 5 cups hot strong coffee
> ½ cup heavy cream, whipped very firm and chilled

1. Prewarm 6 7-ounce goblets by filling them with hot water, draining, and shaking dry. Into each goblet put 1 or 2 tea-

spoons of sugar, depending on taste, and a 1-ounce jigger (or less) of whiskey.

2. Fill each glass about three-quarters full of hot coffee. Carefully float a large dollop of the whipped cream on top of each serving. Drink the hot coffee through the cool cream.

Cocktail Parties
and Buffets

Cocktail parties are great for mixing, and I'm not speaking of drinks alone. Guests arrive anticipating a short hour or so of animated conversation and make the most of it. They move about the room, striking up new conversations, drinking a bit, eating a bit, and then they're off. The large cocktail party is, for the most part, a brief, spirited social function that rewards both the giver and guests.

No matter how large the party, don't try to use it as a catchall for all your outstanding social I.O.U.'s. Include some, of course, but if the party is to zing along, the guest list must be as carefully constructed as one for an intimate dinner party.

Since large cocktail parties are not everyday affairs, one often is at sea about how much liquor to order. You can probably count on three drinks per customer but turn to your liquor dealer for guidance; he has a good idea of what the current drinking patterns are and can help you plan accordingly. Cocktail vogues do change. Ten years ago a bottle of white wine was a rarity on the bar; now it is ordered by the case. Kirs (white wine and crème de cassis) were terrifically popular for a while, but now red wine and old-fashioned mixed cocktails are returning to the fore.

A fifth of liquor will yield 16 jiggers 1½ ounces each. Sherry does not go quite as far—only 12 2-ounce servings.

Supply the bar with both dry and sweet vermouth, the usual assortment of hard liquors, soft drinks, and plenty of soda, tonic water, and a large pitcher of tap water.

Measure all alcohol; don't trust your eye, unless you think tipsy guests are fun. Watch out for guests who show signs of overimbibing and, if they order a refill, water it heavily.

It's best to be prepared with the fixings for all sorts of mixed drinks: maraschino cherries, pitted green olives, pickled onions, lemon zest and slices, half slices of oranges, lime slices, and bitters. Provide lots and lots of paper napkins, especially in the summer when glasses sweat more. Make or buy much more ice than you think necessary; better to have leftovers melt in the sink than run short.

Depending on the size and layout of rooms, it is usually advisable to set up a second bar in another room when the guest list excedes 10 or 12. A heavy crockery bowl or wine bucket can be used as an auxiliary ice bucket. Duplicate most of the bottles and equipment of the main bar, though less popular items such as Campari need only be stocked at one. Don't forget to place wastebaskets by both bars for bottle caps and paper napkins.

Always provide plenty of food to stave off the effects of the alcohol. If a food table is set up, place it at some distance from the bar to avoid traffic pileups.

And remember—one sure way to end a cocktail party is to close the bar.

The host or hostess who invites people for cocktails often plans on offering some solid food at the end of the happy hour. For this reason, recipes to cover both categories are included in this section. Such items as Curried Peanuts and Pizzettes are finger-food tidbits to accompany cocktails. Next there is a quintet of ideas that can bridge the cocktail party and the buffet table. Hearty soups follow because they provide a worry-proof scheme for serving food that will stick to the ribs but does not require any last-minute fussing. The last set of recipes is meant for plate service from a buffet table. The meat dishes are cooked with vegetables, making a complete main course on one platter—an efficient and delicious device that allows various flavors to mingle. Desserts are often eliminated at buffet parties, but in other chapters the reader will find a number of confections that could sweetly end the meal. A frozen soufflé is included here simply because of its size—this recipe has been adapted to serve as many as fourteen people.

CURRIED PEANUTS

Unsalted and unroasted peanuts are needed for this snappy cocktail tidbit. You can usually find them in Chinese shops or health-food stores. Plan to fry the nuts at least a day before serving to allow the flavor to deepen.

Makes 1 cup

2 tablespoons oil
2 to 3 tablespoons curry powder
1 cup raw peanuts

1. Line a baking sheet with paper towels. Pour the oil into a heavy skillet that will hold the peanuts in a single layer. Add the curry powder and stir for half a minute to amalgamate the oil and spice, then add the nuts. Over medium-high heat, stir the nuts with a wooden spoon until they turn a dark golden color. Using a slotted spoon, transfer the nuts to the baking sheet. Pat with paper towels to remove excess surface oil.

NOTE: It is best not to try to fry a double batch. A frying pan large enough to hold them in a single layer will have cold spots where the pan is not in contact with the burner.

CHINESE DRIED NUTS

Walnuts or pecans are traditionally used for this special treatment. It may seem strange to soak these nuts in boiling water, but it does wonders, removing the edge of natural bitterness and giving the kernels a plush texture that cannot be achieved in any other fashion. I find that the flavor seems to develop if they are allowed to stand for a day or two before serving.

Makes 2 cups

2 cups perfect pecan or walnut halves
2 teaspoons oil
½ teaspoon coarse salt
1½ tablespoons sugar (approximately)

1. Put the nuts in a heatproof bowl and pour enough boiling water over them to cover by about 1 inch; cover the bowl and put aside for 45 minutes.
Preheat oven to 300 degrees.
2. Drain the nuts well and pat dry. Line a baking sheet with several thicknesses of paper towels and scatter the nuts over the towels in a single layer; do not allow them to double up. Bake the nuts for 30 minutes. Turn the baking sheet and reduce the heat to 250 degrees, and bake the nuts for an additional 15 minutes or until they are completely dried with just a hint of moisture in the centers.
3. Heat the oil in a heavy skillet or wok, add the nuts, and stir with a wooden spoon until all the nuts are glossy from the oil. Reduce the heat, sprinkle with salt, and stir again. While stirring, slowly sprinkle in the sugar, using more or less to suit your taste. (I find 1½ tablespoons gives a good balance for a sweet-and-sour effect.) Keep stirring the nuts until the sugar has carmelized (turned from a white sugary appearance to a dark and transparent coating on the nuts). Remove the nuts from the skillet at once or the caramel will harden and cause the nuts to stick to the pan. Cool and store in a well-covered container.

PEPPER CHEESE

Herb and pepper cheeses are made both in France and in America. Though they are good spreads on crackers, the cook can also use them to zesty advantage. Use some on top of tomato halves for broiling; smear a dollop on a grilled steak and give it a quick flash under the broiler to create a pepper steak. But instead of buying the cheese ready-made, make pepper cheese yourself and alter the flavorings to suit your taste. Try a touch of garlic or a hint of chopped ginger. I like what brandy does to the rich cheese. If you prefer, the brandy can be omitted; then double the quantity of milk.

Makes about 1 cup

8 ounces cream cheese, at room temperature
1 tablespoon milk
1 tablespoon brandy
2 teaspoons cracked pepper, or to taste

Whip all the ingredients together with an electric beater until well amalgamated. Scrape the pepper cheese into a serving bowl, cover closely, and refrigerate until needed.

CHUTNEY SPREAD

Regular, full-fat cream cheese can be used for this zesty spread. But if it is being served with aperitifs before dinner, I urge you to use the less-caloric, light cream cheese.

Make 1¹/₂ cups

8 ounces light cream cheese
1 tablespoon milk
1 tablespoon raspberry vinegar
large pinch cumin
¹/₃ cup chutney, chopped
Belgian endive or toast rounds

1. With a fork, mash the cream cheese in a bowl to soften it a little. Add the milk, raspberry vinegar, and cumin and work them into the cheese. Add the chutney and thoroughly blend it into the cheese base. Cover and refrigerate for at least 1 day.
2. Spread the flavored cream cheese on toast rounds or over most of the inside curve of the endive leaves, leaving the green tip plain.

TAPENADE

The name of this tangy spread comes from the old Provençal word for capers (*tapènes*), an important ingredient in the making of *tapenade*. This puree is rarely found outside Provence, probably because of the laborious method of its preparation. Today, the traditional mortar and pestle can be replaced by the food processor or even a blender. Serve the *tapenade* spread on melba toast.

Makes 2 cups

1½ cups oil-cured black olives, pitted
¼ to ½ cup olive oil
2 tablespoons lemon juice
2 tablespoons brandy
1 can (3¼ ounces) tuna fish, in oil
1 bottle (3¼ ounces) capers, drained
1 ounce anchovy fillets, in oil
1 garlic clove, chopped
1½ tablespoons English mustard powder
½ teaspoon finely ground black pepper
large pinch ground cloves
large pinch ground ginger
large pinch freshly grated nutmeg

1. Put the olives into the bowl of a food processor equipped with the steel knife. With the motor running, pour ¼ cup of the olive oil into the container. Turn off the motor and add the rest of the ingredients.
2. Process the mixture to a smooth paste. Add the remaining oil if desired. Taste and correct the seasoning if necessary. Scrape the paste into a container, cover, and refrigerate. (It will keep for a week or can be frozen.)

NOTE: If an electric blender is used, combine the oil, lemon juice, and brandy before slowly adding the remaining ingredients. Some blenders may require more oil than indicated above.

BLUE CHEESE NUGGETS

Wheat germ may seem a strange coating for these little cheese balls. Ground nuts certainly can be used, but I feel there is already enough richness in the pungent morsels.

Makes about 40 nuggets

> 4 ounces blue-veined cheese
> 1 tablespoon heavy cream
> 2 teaspoons brandy
> 2 tablespoons coarsely ground walnuts
> 6 tablespoons wheat germ

1. Cream together the cheese, cream, and brandy. Stir in the walnuts and chill the mixture.
2. Line a dish with wax paper. Pour the wheat germ into a small saucer. Roll about ½ teaspoon of the cheese mixture at a time between the palms of your hands into a small round ball, roll each piece in the wheat germ, and place it on the dish. Refrigerate nuggets for at least one hour. (These nuggets also freeze well.)
3. To serve, plunge a toothpick into each cheese nugget and arrange on a platter with the toothpicks standing up.

MARINATED BLACK OLIVES

Though oil-cured Mediterranean-style olives work best, almost any kind of olive can be used with this marinade, even California's mild specimens.

2½ cups black olives (2 5¾-ounce cans)
1 to 1½ cups olive oil
¼ cup white wine
2 garlic cloves, bruised
2 basil sprigs or 2 teaspoons dried basil

1. Rinse the olives under cold running water and place in a jar that will hold them compactly. In another jar, shake together ½ cup olive oil, wine, garlic, and dried basil, if using.
2. Pour the marinade over the olives and, if using fresh basil, tuck in the sprigs. Add just enough oil to cover the olives. Cover tightly and let stand at room temperature for 1 or 2 days, then refrigerate for at least 1 week.
3. To serve, drain the olives and discard the basil sprigs and garlic.

CITRUS-SPICED OLIVES

Several differently flavored olives make an interesting offering on a buffet table or antipasto tray. As a counterpoint to the herb-scented black olives in the preceding recipe, try this hot citrus-sparked variation.

3 cups green olives
½ lemon, thinly sliced and seeded
3 thin slices thin-skinned orange, seeded
½ teaspoon hot red pepper flakes
½ to ¾ cup olive oil

1. Rinse the olives, drain very well, and put in a mixing bowl. Cut the lemon and orange slices, including the rinds, into small pieces and scatter them over the olives. Add the pepper flakes and ¼ cup of the olive oil. Mix well with your hands to coat all of the olives with the oil and pepper flakes.
2. Transfer the olives and all of the flavorings to a jar with a tight-fitting lid. Pour in enough oil to completely cover the

olives by about ½ inch. Seal well, let stand at room temperature for 1 day, and then refrigerate for a week before serving.

TUNA-PECAN TERRINE

If you are having cocktails or just sipping white wine, this rich
but not assertive tuna paste will be a perfect accompaniment.
It needs a full day for the flavors to marry well, which means
one less last-minute thing to fuss with. It will keep in the
refrigerator for a week.

Makes 2 cups

1 6½-ounce can tuna, in oil
3 tablespoons brandy
¼ teaspoon sesame seed oil
dash of Tabasco
2 hard-boiled eggs, quartered
6 ounces cream cheese
¼ cup pecans, coarsely chopped
1 tablespoon capers, rinsed and well drained
Garnish: 2 pecan halves, capers, or a fresh herb sprig

1. Place the tuna with its oil, brandy, sesame seed oil, and
Tabasco in the blender or food processor and puree. Gradually
add the eggs and then the cream cheese and process until very
smooth.
2. Stir in the nuts and capers. Scrape mixture into a 2-cup
dish or crock. Refrigerate for 24 hours and garnish as desired
at serving time. Pass with small toasts or crackers.

STUDENT'S PÂTÉ

I can't explain the name of this amazing pâté, since it came to
me from a Johns Hopkins professor who happens to be an

excellent cook. His note with the recipe read, "Don't knock it till you try it." I was very skeptical, indeed, until I tried it.

Makes 2 cups

¼ pound butter (1 stick)
1 onion, chopped
2 garlic cloves, chopped
1 8-ounce liverwurst, cut into chunks
2 tablespoons brandy
½ teaspoon nutmeg
¼ teaspoon allspice
salt and pepper

1. Melt the butter in a skillet, add the onions, cover, and simmer about 10 minutes or until they are soft; do not allow them to brown. Add the garlic, liverwurst, brandy, nutmeg, allspice, salt, and pepper. Cook the mixture over brisk heat, stirring and breaking up the liverwurst, until the liverwurst seems to have absorbed some of the butter; this should take between 5 and 10 minutes.
2. Transfer the contents of the skillet to a blender or food processor and process until the mixture is very smooth. Taste for seasonings and correct if necessary. Scrape the puree into a 2-cup mold and chill. Student's pâté is best if refrigerated for 2 or 3 days before serving.

PARMESAN PUFFS

This hot cocktail tidbit can be whipped together with ingredients that are usually on hand. For onion-shy people, the recipe can be made with chives. I urge using the onion, however, since its assertiveness stands up better to the rich mayonnaise.

Makes about 25 1-inch toast rounds

½ cup mayonnaise
⅔ cup freshly grated Parmesan cheese
¼ teaspoon cognac
large pinch curry
salt and pepper
2 tablespoons chopped chives or 1 tablespoon grated
   onion
about 25 1-inch melba toast rounds

1. Mix the mayonnaise with the Parmesan cheese, cognac, curry, salt, and pepper. If using chives, stir them in and mound the mixture on the toast rounds. If using onion, place a large pinch of onion on each of the toast rounds and cover with the mayonnaise-cheese mixture. (The puffs can be prepared ahead and refrigerated for several hours.)
   Preheat the broiler.
2. Place the puffs on a baking sheet. Broil about 5 inches from the heat for 4 to 5 minutes or until the tops are puffed and browned. Serve immediately.

HOT CHEESE-OLIVE PUFFS

There is no way of telling that inside each of these golden cheese nuggets lurks a whole olive. The contrast startles at first, then delights. Because the olives will retain the high temperature for a while, don't serve them right out of the oven. Cocktail onions or whole almonds can be used in place of the olives for a different effect.

Makes about 25 puffs

1 cup shredded cheddar cheese
3 tablespoons soft butter
⅔ cup flour
1 teaspoon salt
½ teaspoon paprika

½ teaspoon brandy
½ teaspoon Worcestershire sauce
25 green olives stuffed with pimiento (approximately)

1. Blend the cheese and butter together, then stir in the flour, salt, paprika, brandy, and Worcestershire sauce. Make certain all the ingredients are thoroughly mixed. Chill for at least ½ hour to firm the dough. (The cheese dough can be made a day or so in advance, then removed from the refrigerator just long enough to soften a bit before continuing.)
Preheat oven to 400 degrees.
2. Wrap a teaspoon of cheese dough around each olive, completely covering it. Arrange nuggets on an ungreased cookie sheet and bake for 10 to 15 minutes or until nicely browned. Cool for 10 minutes before serving.

MUSHROOM HOTBITS

For all its panache, this hot cocktail treat is very easy to put together. It looks pretty and has a zesty flavor, both of which belie its simplicity. The secret lies in the herb-and-garlic-scented cheese such as Boursin or Rondele, available in small boxes from France or the United States. I find the French version smoother.

Makes 30 bite-size pieces

30 mushroom caps (about ½ pound with stems)
olive oil
3 ounces herb-and-garlic cheese (about ½ cup)
3 to 4 tablespoons heavy cream
15 cherry tomatoes

1. Stem the mushrooms and reserve stems for another use. Rinse the caps and brush the outsides with olive oil. In a small bowl mash the cheese with a fork, then stir in enough cream to

make a soft mixture. Stuff the mushroom caps with about a scant teaspoon of the cheese (more or less depending on size of caps).

2. Cut the cherry tomatoes in half crosswise and press one into each filled mushroom cap, cut-side down. Place the stuffed caps on a baking sheet.

Preheat oven to 375 degrees.

3. Bake for about 10 minutes or just until the mushroom caps and tomatoes are warmed a little and the cheese begins to melt. If baked too long the tomatoes will go limp. Serve immediately.

ENGLISH RABBIT

If melted cheddar cheese is turned into a Welsh rabbit, why can't Stilton cheese serve for an English Rabbit? Don't spread the cheese mixture too thickly on the toast rounds; once heated, blue-veined cheeses are stronger.

Makes about 72 1-inch toasts

4 ounces Stilton or other blue-veined cheese
¼ cup sour cream
½ teaspoon brandy
dash of Tabasco
black pepper
about 72 Melba toast rounds

1. Using a fork, mash the cheese in a bowl. Add the sour cream, brandy, a good dash of Tabasco, and a lot of freshly ground black pepper. Continue working with the fork to thoroughly blend all ingredients. (The cheese mixture can be closely covered and refrigerated for several days.)

Preheat broiler.

2. Spread a thin coating of the cheese on the toast rounds,

then place on a baking sheet and broil for a minute or so. The cheese should be bubbly and flecked with golden spots. Serve immediately.

OYSTERS À L'ESCARGOT

If you have kitchen and serving help during a cocktail party, use these garlic-scented oysters to cause a sensation. Otherwise, serve them as a treat to dinner guests. Four oysters make a perfect first-course serving. The success of the dish lies in not overbaking the bivalves, which causes them to toughen. A bed of coarse salt in the baking pan is strongly recommended to stabilize the oysters during the baking. Also, the salt becomes hot in the oven and helps keep the oysters hot, which means the pan can be placed on a buffet table.

Makes 30 oysters

Snail Butter:
   ½ pound butter, softened
   2 shallots, finely chopped (about 2 tablespoons)
   4 garlic cloves, finely chopped (about 1 tablespoon)
   juice of ½ lemon
   large pinch of cayenne
   salt and pepper
30 oysters in the shell
coarse salt (optional)

1. Cream together the soft butter and seasonings. Refrigerate or freeze until needed.
   Preheat oven to 500 degrees.
2. Bring the snail butter to room temperature. Scrub the oysters well and place them on a large jelly roll pan. A baking sheet cannot be used because the oysters exude too much juice. Line pan with a bed of coarse salt, if using. Place the oysters in the pan or in the salt bed, round side down. Bake for

about 3 minutes or just until you can see the oyster shells beginning to separate.

3. With an oyster knife or other sturdy knife, pry off the top flat shell, cutting the oyster muscle if it is connected. Discard the shell.

4. Top each oyster with about 1½ teaspoons of the snail butter. Try to cover as much of the surface as possible; as the butter melts, it will bathe the entire oyster surface. Return to the hot oven for about 2 minutes or just until the butter has melted. Serve at once with small oyster forks.

PIZZETTES

Pizza seems to be eaten at almost every hour of the day except the cocktail hour. Naturally, long, limp slices won't do as finger food, but small 2-inch pizzas will prove a hit. The dough is very easy to make, either by hand or in a food processor. The list of suggested toppings is just a beginning; use your imagination.

Makes about 26 2-inch pizzettes

2 teaspoons dry yeast
¾ cup lukewarm water
1 tablespoon olive oil
2 cups flour
¼ teaspoon salt

1. Put the yeast, water, and olive oil in the bowl of a food processor, cover, and let stand for 2 minutes. Add the flour and salt; process just until the mixture becomes a ball and stop the machine immediately. If you lack a food processor, dissolve the yeast in the water and oil for about 3 minutes. Measure the flour and salt into a mixing bowl, add the yeast liquid, and stir

with a wooden spoon until the dough begins to take shape, then continue blending by hand.

2. Pull the dough onto a floured board. Knead the dough for 1 minute, shape into a ball, place in a mixing bowl, and cover. Put the bowl in a warm spot to allow the dough to double in bulk. This should take about 1 hour.

Preheat oven to 450 degrees.

3. Pinch off about 3 tablespoons of dough at a time and flatten into a 2-inch round. (Some cooks like to moisten their fingertips with a little olive oil while working with the dough.) Top rounds with any desired ingredients. Bake the pizzettes on an oiled baking sheet for about 10 minutes or until the crust is crisp and the topping hot. Serve at once.

Suggested Pizzette Toppings:
Tomato Sauce (page 244) reduced in half over high heat.
Tomato Sauce and Mozzarella Cheese
Tomato Sauce and Goat Cheese
Tomato Sauce with Fried Onions and Mushrooms
Tomato Sauce with Fried Onions and Anchovies
Tomato Sauce with Sliced Sausage and Sautéed Green Peppers
Grated Cheddar Cheese mixed with Sautéed Red Peppers
Grated Cheddar Cheese mixed with Black Olive Slices and
   White Wine
Tuna Fish mixed with Ricotta and Capers
Tuna Fish mixed with Ricotta and Chopped Pimiento
Ricotta mixed with grated Parmesan Cheese, slivers of Cured
   Ham, and Sautéed Onion
Make up your own!

"CAKE" AUX OLIVES (OLIVE CAKE)

Don't blanch. This is not a sweet cake with olives. Actually, in French culinary language the term "cake" does not refer as much to the batter mixture as to the loaf shape it is baked in.

Country people in France enjoyed this savory snack long before the cocktail came along. Not only is it perfect with cocktails but also on the buffet table or tucked inside the picnic hamper. Oh yes, *gâteau* is what they call a real cake.

Makes 1 8^1/$_2$ × 4^1/$_2$ × 2^1/$_2$-inch loaf

2¼ cups flour
4 eggs
½ cup olive oil
⅓ cup white wine
1 teaspoon baking powder
¼ pound Gruyère cheese in 1 slice, cut into tiny dice
¼ pound ham in 1 slice, cut into tiny dice
about 20 black olives, preferably oil-cured (⅔ cup when pitted and cut into small pieces)
about 20 green olives (⅔ cup when pitted and cut into small pieces)

Preheat oven to 375 degrees.

1. Put the flour in a mixing bowl, make a well in the center and place the eggs and ¼ cup of the olive oil in the well. Beat the eggs and oil together with a wooden spoon while adding the remaining ¼ cup of oil, leaving flour around edges of bowl.

2. In a small bowl stir the wine into the baking powder to dissolve it, then add this to the liquid ingredients in the center of the flour. Slowly incorporate the flour into the liquid ingredients and beat well for several minutes. Add the cheese, ham, and olives and mix again.

3. Oil a loaf pan and place a piece of parchment paper in the bottom, then oil the paper. Spoon the thick batter into the pan and bake for 10 minutes. Reduce the temperature to 350 degrees and continue baking for another 30 to 35 minutes or until a toothpick plunged in the center comes out clean. Cool before turning out of mold.

BALTIMORE'S BAKED POTATO SKINS

I can't imagine why this cocktail snack became identified with Baltimore, a city far removed from any potato farms. But, thank goodness, they knew a good thing when they saw it. Do not confuse these crisp morsels with the type now sold in restaurants that contain a good deal of the potato flesh plus other fixings. Those are a meal; these are a snack. The proportions in this recipe are up to you.

> baked potatoes
> melted butter
> salt and pepper

Preheat oven to 450 degrees.
1. Cut the baked potatoes in half lengthwise. Scoop out all of the white flesh and reserve it for another use. Cut the potato skins into strips about 1 inch wide and place them on a baking sheet. Brush liberally with the butter and sprinkle with salt and pepper.
2. Bake the potato skins until they are very crisp. Serve hot.

MARINATED SMOKED COD

This pungent little dish is very easy to make and never fails to please. Start it a week before you need it.

Serves 12

> 1 pound smoked cod
> ¾ to 1 cup oil
> 2 onions, thinly sliced

1. Cut the cod into fillets about ¼ inch thick. Oil a glass or ceramic gratin dish and arrange half the fillets in a layer.

Spread half the onions over the fish, then dribble half the oil over the onions.

2. Repeat with the other half of the ingredients for a second layer. Cover tightly and leave at room temperature for 6 to 12 hours, then store in a cool place or refrigerate for one week or more. Baste occasionally with oil in the dish.

3. To serve, lift the fillets out of the oil and arrange on a serving platter. Some of the onions can be scattered over the cod; they will have softened and mellowed a little in the oil.

CHICKEN AND CHICKEN LIVER MOUSSE IN ASPIC

Even in hot weather there need be no fear of the aspic collapsing. This is not an unmolded affair, but layers of moist chicken pieces and a creamy mousse encased in a well-flavored aspic. It is equally fine eating even in the dead of winter.

Serves 8 to 10

2 quarts water
1 medium onion, quartered
3 carrots, cut into chunks
leafy top from a celery rib
6 sprigs parsley
2 chicken bouillon cubes
salt and pepper
1 4-pound chicken
2 egg whites, lightly beaten (optional)
1 to 3 tablespoons gelatin
¼ cup Madeira or port
8 tablespoons butter
1 pound chicken livers
½ teaspoon thyme
2 tablespoons sour cream or *crème fraîche*
1 tablespoon brandy

1. Measure the water into a large pot and add the onion, carrots, celery, parsley, bouillon cubes, salt, pepper, and the giblets and neck from the chicken. Bring the water to a slow boil, cover, and simmer for 20 minutes.

2. Add the chicken to the stock plus enough water to almost cover the chicken. Cover and simmer for 50 minutes, periodically removing with a skimmer any scum that floats to the top. Drain the chicken and let it cool, then cover with plastic wrap and refrigerate. Strain the cooking stock and reserve 5 or 6 of the carrot pieces.

3. The stock should now be clarified for a better presentation although this step is optional. Bring the stock to a slow simmer, add the lightly beaten egg whites, and whisk vigorously until stock comes to a boil. Turn off the heat and let the stock stand for 10 minutes. Repeat process, bringing the stock to a boil and letting it stand. Place a strainer over a deep bowl or pot, line it with a wet linen dish towel (no holes, please), and ladle the stock through the towel. Discard any remaining vegetables. Measure the clarified stock.

4. Test the consistency of the stock by chilling a few tablespoons in a saucer for about 15 minutes. For this recipe the aspic should be firm and remain separated when cut into pieces. If the sample of stock is only loosely jelled, use 1½ tablespoons of gelatin for every 4 cups of clarified stock. Soak the gelatin in the Madeira or port. Reheat the stock and stir the softened gelatin into the hot stock until dissolved. Cool and retest.

5. Remove membranes and connective tissue from the chicken livers. In a heavy skillet, heat 2 tablespoons of the butter until foamy. Add the chicken livers and cook, turning frequently; sprinkle with thyme and salt and pepper to taste. Cook no longer than 2 or 3 minutes, as the livers should remain pink in the center.

6. Transfer the livers to a food processor and puree or force them through the fine blade of a food mill to eliminate all membranes. Place in a mixing bowl. Melt the remaining 6 tablespoons of butter and add it to the livers along with the sour cream or *crème fraîche,* brandy, and ¼ cup of the aspic stock. Stir well and set aside to cool.

7. Select a deep platter and pour in enough aspic to cover the bottom; refrigerate until set. Meanwhile, remove the skin and bones from the chicken and tear the meat into bite-size pieces.

8. Spread two-thirds of the chicken liver mousse over the set aspic in the platter and chill for at least 30 minutes. Pile the chicken pieces over the mousse, smooth the top, and cover with the remaining mousse. Chill again for at least 30 minutes.

9. Spoon more aspic over the mousse and chill; repeat this procedure as many times as necessary to form a thick coating of aspic. Before applying the final coat or two of aspic, slice the reserved carrot pieces into neat rounds and place them around the rim of the platter and in the center of the mousse with a small sprig of parsley. Chill until serving time.

10. Serve directly from the platter, cutting the aspic into squares or pie-shaped wedges, depending on the shape of the platter.

SPINACH-BASIL TERRINE

Summer's fresh basil makes a heady flavor difference in this terrine. Still, it is too good to pass up the rest of the year. Substitute dried basil, using one tablespoon in each of the two layers.

Makes about 3¹/₂ pounds

1 pound calf's liver
2 tablespoons olive oil
¼ cup brandy
1 teaspoon thyme
1½ pounds pork shoulder, ground
1 pound turkey breast, ground
1 medium onion, chopped
2 tablespoons butter
2 garlic cloves, minced
½ cup white wine
¼ cup bread crumbs

2 teaspoons salt
1 teaspoon pepper
1 egg, beaten
2 cups basil leaves (or 2 tablespoons dried basil)
¼ pound spinach
2 bay leaves
caul or oil

1. Remove all the nerves from the liver, cut the meat into ½-inch-wide strips, and place them in a small bowl. Add the olive oil, brandy, and thyme and mix well with your hands. Cover and refrigerate overnight.
Preheat oven to 375 degrees.
2. Combine the ground pork and turkey in a large mixing bowl. In a covered skillet, sauté the onion in the butter for 5 minutes. Add the garlic and simmer 1 minute more. Scrape the cooked onions and garlic over the ground meats.
3. Lift the liver strips out of the marinade and reserve. Pour the marinade and white wine into the onion skillet and boil briskly to reduce by half. Pour this wine reduction over the meats. Add the bread crumbs, salt, and pepper and mix well with your hands. Add the egg and mix again. Fry a teaspoon of the forcemeat mixture, cool, and taste for seasonings; correct if necessary.
4. Select an 8-cup terrine mold. If using caul to line it, see the note below; otherwise oil the mold. Scoop in about a third of the forcemeat and smooth it into a neat layer; tap the mold sharply on the counter. Reserve 2 of the largest basil leaves; layer in half the basil leaves over the forcemeat (or sprinkle 1 tablespoon dried basil), then top with half the liver strips. Cover the liver strips with half the spinach leaves and press all down firmly. Repeat with another third of the forcemeat and the rest of the basil, liver strips, and spinach, and then a final layer of forcemeat. Keep tapping the mold against the counter as you add layers. On top of the final meat layer, press the 2 reserved basil leaves and 2 bay leaves. Either smear oil over the surface, or pull up the excess caul.
5. Cover the mold with aluminum foil, place the lid on the

mold, and, with a skewer, poke a hole into the foil through the vent hole. Put the mold in a gratin dish or roasting pan and pour in enough hot water to reach halfway up the side of the mold. Bake for about 1½ hours or until a meat thermometer registers 160 degrees.

6. Remove the terrine mold from the water bath, uncover and let stand for 20 minutes. Place 4 or 5 pounds of weights on top and allow to cool. Refrigerate overnight with the weights in place. Remove the weights and refrigerate for at least 3 or 4 days before serving.

NOTE: Caul, the fatty membrane from the stomach of a pig, is available from specialty butchers either fresh, dry-salted, or frozen. Always rinse caul well; dry-salted caul should be soaked in several changes of water over a few hours before using.

VEGETABLE SOUP WITH MEATBALLS AND PASTA

It is so easy to invite friends to stay on after a cocktail party when a big pot of hearty soup is ready. This is only one steaming example that can be made a day or so ahead of time and reheated when needed.

Serves 10 to 12

12 cups beef broth
6 celery ribs, including leaves, chopped
2 carrots, chopped
2 teaspoons oregano
2 cups canned tomatoes
1 cup fine pasta, or spaghetti broken into bits
grated Parmesan cheese

Meatballs:
4 slices bread, preferably a few days old

146

2 pounds ground beef
2 eggs, lightly beaten
2 teaspoons Worcestershire sauce
2 teaspoons salt
pepper to taste

1. Pour the beef broth in a large pot and add the celery, carrots, oregano, and tomatoes, crushing the pulp with your hands as you put them in. Bring the broth to a boil and simmer for 15 minutes.

2. Meanwhile, prepare the meatballs. Soak the bread in water and squeeze out the moisture. Mix the bread with the ground beef and the lightly beaten eggs, Worcestershire sauce, salt, and pepper. Knead the meat mixture with your fingertips until all the ingredients are well blended. Form into 1-inch-diameter-meatballs.

3. Add the meatballs to the simmering stock. Once all of the meatballs are in the pot, adjust the heat to keep the liquid just gently simmering. Cook for about 15 minutes. (The soup can be prepared to this point ahead of time.)

4. Reheat the soup to simmering point if it has been cooled. Add the pasta and cook another 3 to 5 minutes, or until the pasta is *al dente*. Serve in deep bowls and pass the grated Parmesan cheese.

MINESTRONE

Minestrone can be a variable feast if you adjust vegetables and quantities to suit the season and your taste. The Italian name means "thick soup," so don't be timid when adding your market-basket selections. If you have time, substitute dried white beans for the canned beans since they add a richness to the cooking broth. They require 1 hour of soaking in boiling water and another 1 hour of cooking. One cup of marrow, Great Northern, or white kidney beans is sufficient.

Serves 8 to 10

2 tablespoons olive oil
1/4 pound bacon, preferably in 1 piece, cut into 1/2-inch
    cubes
1 medium onion, thinly sliced
3 carrots, thinly sliced
4 ribs celery, thinly sliced
1 leek, thinly sliced
4 small or 2 medium zucchini, cut into 1/2-inch pieces
10 cups water
2 garlic cloves, minced
2 teaspoons salt
1/2 teaspoon pepper
1 teaspoon basil
1 herb bouquet (6 parsley sprigs and 2 bay leaves tied
    together)
1-pound can plum tomatoes, not drained
1 1/2 cups beef broth
2 beef bouillon cubes
a 1-pound-4-ounce can white kidney beans *(cannellini)*
1 cup frozen peas (about half a 10-ounce package)
2 to 3 ounces spaghetti, broken in pieces, or elbow
    macaroni (1/2 to 1 cup)
grated Parmesan cheese

1. Heat olive oil in a large soup pot, add bacon, and fry slowly until the pieces are lightly browned. Remove the bacon with a skimmer and reserve. Add the sliced onion, carrots, celery, leek, and zucchini and fry gently for about 10 minutes or until the vegetables begin to wilt.

2. Add plain water or the partially cooked dried beans with 10 cups of their cooking liquid, plus garlic, salt, pepper, basil, herb bouquet, tomatoes with liquid (squeeze pulp through your fingers), beef broth, and beef cubes. Return bacon to the pot. Partially cover and cook for 30 minutes. Discard the herb bouquet.

3. If canned beans are used, add them now along with peas and spaghetti or macaroni. Cover and cook another 10 minutes.

4. Serve in deep bowls and pass the Parmesan cheese to be sprinkled on top.

HOME-STYLE BOUILLABAISSE

There are all sorts of legends about the kinds of fish necessary to make a true bouillabaisse. The ground rules were laid down around Marseilles, where some of these "essential" fish swim, but 50 miles farther down the Mediterranean coast the requirements are ignored. There is no reason in the world why a first-class, if unconventional, bouillabaisse cannot be prepared anywhere fish is sold. The secret is a judiciously flavored broth, not some mysterious combination of creatures from the sea.

Serves 8

½ cup olive oil
3 onions, thinly sliced
3 potatoes, peeled, cut in half, sliced ¼ inch thick
2 ribs celery, sliced into ¼-inch pieces
5 garlic cloves, peeled and mashed
1 2-pound can plum tomatoes
2 to 3 cups clam juice
2 cups white wine
1 2-ounce can anchovy fillets
2 teaspoons fennel seeds
½ teaspoon oregano
½ teaspoon basil
½ teaspoon thyme
¼ teaspoon saffron
2 tablespoons tomato paste
pepper
2 tablespoons anise-flavored liqueur (Ouzo, Pernod, or Arak)
2 pounds fish in 1 piece (haddock, cod, or other firm white fish)
1 pound mussels (see Moules Marinières, pages 191–92, for cleaning instructions)

1. In a large pot, heat the oil and add the onions. Cover and simmer while preparing potatoes, celery, and garlic.

2. Add the vegetables, including the tomatoes, crushing the pulp with your hands as you put them in. Pour in 2 cups of clam juice and add all remaining ingredients except fish and mussels. Cover and simmer for 30 minutes or until the potatoes are soft.

3. Taste the broth for seasoning and correct if necessary, adding salt or extra clam juice. Add the fish, re-cover, and simmer until the flesh turns white and separates easily, about 10 minutes per 1 inch of thickness. Add the mussels for the last 2 or 3 minutes of cooking, simmering them just until their shells open.

4. Lift the piece of white fish out of the bouillabaisse stock, let cool slightly, then remove the skin and bones. Flake the fish into good-sized chunks and return to the pot to reheat. If bouillabaisse is made in advance, add the mussels when reheating just before serving.

SMOKED HADDOCK CHOWDER

There is a whole soup pot full of reasons for planning a party around this special chowder: it's ready in well under an hour; it requires no last-minute shopping since the smoked fish can be kept in the refrigerator for a week; it's economical since just 1½ pounds of this strongly flavored fish will make a stew to serve 10 people; and it's a good bet your guests haven't had it before.

Serves 10

3 medium onions, chopped
3 stalks celery, thinly sliced
3 medium potatoes, peeled and cut into thick slices
1 quart milk

salt and pepper
1½ pounds smoked haddock
1 cup heavy cream

1. Put the onions and celery in a soup pot, cover with water, put a lid on the pot, and simmer gently for 10 minutes. Add the potatoes and continue cooking until the vegetables are almost done, about 15 minutes.

2. Add the milk, salt, pepper, and haddock (cut fish into 2 or 3 pieces if it is large). Simmer gently for 20 to 25 minutes or until the vegetables and fish are completely cooked; turn off the heat. Remove haddock and cool. Then remove the tough skin and bones and flake the fish into large chunks.

3. Stir the cream into the soup, return the fish pieces, and taste for seasoning; correct if necessary. Cook for 5 minutes more. (If preparing the soup in advance, return the flaked fish to the pot, but do not add the cream until reheating the chowder.)

MIXED MEAT-AND-VEGETABLE ROAST

This recipe is meant to be a guideline only. Quantities can be varied and vegetables and meat cuts changed according to seasonal availability or to suit your taste. There is only one rule to follow: select meats and vegetables that bake in approximately the same length of time. When tiny new potatoes can be found, add them whole; larger specimens must be cut in quarters. Baby carrots should be left whole, but older ones should be cut into 1-inch pieces. Other meat possibilities are veal chops, split Rock Cornish hens, thick slices of turkey breast, Canadian bacon, or eye-of-round. I like the addition of a small bit of smoked meat; smoked pork is included here, but a sausage link will do just as well. One word of caution: if you plan to feed more than 8 people, make sure you have a large baking pan.

Serves 8

1 pound ground beef
¼ cup chopped onion
1 teaspoon prepared mustard
salt and pepper
1 egg, beaten
2½ pounds chicken pieces
1 pound smoked pork chops
4 or 5 potatoes, cut in quarters
4 or 5 carrots, cut in 1-inch pieces
4 or 5 leeks, white part only, cut in half lengthwise
1 celery rib, broken in half
2 or 3 garlic cloves, mashed but not peeled
1 bay leaf
1 to 1½ cups chicken broth

Preheat oven to 375 degrees.

1. Mix together the ground beef, onion, mustard, and a little salt and pepper until all ingredients are well blended. Add the egg and mix again. Form into 1-inch balls. If desired, meatballs may be browned in a little oil, but this step is not necessary.

2. Arrange the chicken and pork pieces in a large baking pan and scatter the meatballs over them. Around the meats tuck the potatoes, carrots, and leeks. Add the 2 celery pieces, garlic, and bay leaf. Sprinkle with salt and pepper and pour in about 1 cup of chicken broth. Cover the pan tightly and bake for about 1½ hours.

3. Baste from time to time, adding more chicken broth only if necessary to cover the bottom of the pan. Meats and vegetables should not stew in the liquid. Remove the cover for the last 10 minutes of baking. Discard the celery pieces, bay leaf, and garlic before serving.

BEEF AND RED CABBAGE STEW

Stews are perfect for the buffet table. First of all, they are best if made at least a day ahead of time, allowing the flavors to deepen. Second, if made in an attractive enameled cast-iron casserole, the stew can be served in it, insuring greater heat retention. And now with electric hot trays, the simmering pot can sit on the table as long as necessary.

Serves 8 to 10

½ cup oil
4 pounds stewing beef, cut into chunks
4 tablespoons butter
4 onions, thinly sliced
¼ cup tomato paste
1 pound red cabbage, quartered, cored, and shredded
2 pounds Italian plum tomatoes
4 beef bouillon cubes
4 garlic cloves, crushed
juice of 2 lemons
¼ cup brown sugar
1 teaspoon caraway seeds
2 bay leaves
salt and pepper

1. Heat ¼ cup oil in a casserole and when hot add half the meat chunks. Brown the meat quickly on all surfaces over moderately high heat, lift out the meat with a skimmer and reserve in a bowl. Continue with the rest of the meat, adding more oil if necessary. Add the second batch of meat to the bowl.
2. Throw out the oil in the casserole and replace with the butter. Once the butter is melted, add the onions and, using a wooden spoon, scrape up all the coagulated juices from the bottom of the pot. When the onions have turned golden, add

the tomato paste and stir well. Stir in all remaining ingredients, then return the meat to the pot.

3. Simmer slowly until the meat is tender, about 1 hour. Taste for seasonings, which should be a combination of sweet and tart; correct if necessary. Cool, then refrigerate. At serving time, reheat slowly and simmer for an additional 15 minutes.

LAMB CHOP BAKE

This is another excellent buffet dish. The recipe can easily be doubled; simply divide the ingredients between two baking dishes.

Serves 6

5 tablespoons butter (approximately)
6 shoulder lamb chops
3 medium onions, thinly sliced
1 garlic clove, chopped
1 cup beef broth
salt and pepper
4 potatoes

Preheat oven to 400 degrees.

1. Melt 3 tablespoons of butter in a skillet until foamy and hot. Add the chops and brown well on both sides. Add more butter as necessary. Remove browned chops to a dish.

2. Add 1 tablespoon butter to the skillet with the onions and garlic. Stir to loosen coagulated juices from the bottom of the pan and simmer for 2 minutes.

3. Select a baking dish that will hold the chops snugly. Scrape the softened onions and garlic into the dish and pat into a smooth layer. Place the chops on top of the onions. Pour in $1/2$ cup beef broth and sprinkle with salt and pepper. Bake uncovered for 20 minutes.

4. While the chops are baking, peel the potatoes and slice

thinly. Place the potato slices over the chops after they've baked for 20 minutes, covering the meat completely. Pour in the remaining ½ cup of beef broth and again sprinkle with salt and pepper. Return to the oven for about another 20 minutes or until the potatoes are soft. Baste occasionally with the cooking juices. Serve from the baking dish.

SPAGHETTI SQUASH WITH *PESTO*

This dish will be much appreciated on any buffet table, by calorie counters and guests with hearty appetites alike. All that is necessary is a single chafing dish to keep the spaghetti squash warm. Uncooked *pesto* sauce is served at room temperature; when poured over squash, the heat of the squash strands is sufficient to melt the cheese in the sauce. Provide an extra bowl of Parmesan cheese for guests who would like to sprinkle a bit on top.

Serves 10 to 12

   2 spaghetti squashes (about 3 pounds each)
   3 cups *Pesto* Sauce (pages 244–45)

1. With a sturdy fork poke holes into the spaghetti squashes, then boil or steam them for about 30 minutes or just until the skin is tender. (If overcooked, the squash flesh will turn mushy and won't pull out in strands.)

2. Cut the squashes in half, spoon out the seeds and fibers in the center, and pull out strands of the spaghetti squash with a fork and place them into a warm bowl or chafing dish. Serve immediately with *Pesto* Sauce.

NOTE: If the squash must be cooked in advance, pull the strands out of the squash shell, cover, and refrigerate. To reheat, steam over boiling water for about 5 minutes.

POTATO AND MUSSEL SALAD

Teaming mussels with a vegetable is nothing new. In his play *Francillon*, the younger Alexandre Dumas went on at great length describing a salad in which he mixed mussels and potatoes with a few truffles and some champagne. In the kitchen fantasy described below, the vegetable and the mollusk are joined with a Pernod-spiked sauce. Shredded lettuce makes a nice green nest for the mix.

Serves 8 to 10

Potatoes:
- 4 pounds new potatoes
- 4 cups chicken broth
- 2 cups water
- celery leaves from 3 ribs
- 2 cups dry white wine, at room temperature

Dressing:
- ¾ cup olive oil
- 4 tablespoons wine vinegar
- salt and pepper
- ½ teaspoon basil
- ½ teaspoon rosemary
- 1 teaspoon tarragon
- 2 tablespoons anise-flavored liqueur (Pernod, Ouzo, or Arak)

Mussels:
- 6 pounds mussels (or littleneck clams)
- 1 lemon, juice and shell
- lettuce leaves for garnish
- ½ pound shrimp, cooked, shelled, and deveined (optional)

1. Scrub the potatoes well; do not peel. Put the potatoes in a small pot with the chicken broth and water and 1 sprig of celery leaves. Bring to a boil and simmer until the potatoes are soft but not mushy, about 25 minutes. Reserve 2 cups of water and drain off the rest.

2. While the potatoes are cooking, beat together all the ingredients for the dressing. As soon as you can handle the potatoes, peel them and cut into slices about ¼ inch thick. Place the slices in a mixing bowl. Immediately pour ⅔ cup white wine over the potatoes, mix gently, cover, and let stand for 10 minutes. Pour the dressing over the potatoes, mix gently again, cover, and set aside.

3. Scrub and debeard the mussels (see Steamed Mussels, pages 191–92) and put them in a deep pot with the reserved 2 cups of potato water, plus the remaining 1⅓ cups white wine and the remaining celery sprigs. Squeeze in the lemon juice and toss in the lemon shell as well. Cover, bring to a boil over high heat, and cook for a few minutes until the mussel shells open. Cool, then remove the mussels from the shells. (You can reserve the cooking broth for a soup.)

4. Reserve 6 or 8 mussels to garnish the salad and add the rest to the potatoes. Mix carefully and leave at room temperature, covered, for 1 hour. Refrigerate for at least 2 hours.

5. Arrange a bed of lettuce leaves on a serving platter, mound the salad in the center, and arrange the reserved mussels on top. If shrimp are also used, make a circle of them around the mussels.

GRAPEFRUIT RICE

The unexpected tang of grapefruit will quickly awaken plain rice. Thanks to this distinctive flavor, a cool temperature does not diminish its appeal, and you will find it serves well on a cold buffet. If you choose to serve it hot, reduce the yogurt to 4 tablespoons.

Serves 6

2 tablespoons oil
1½ cups long grain rice
1½ cups unsweetened grapefruit juice
1½ cups chicken broth
salt and pepper
6 tablespoons yogurt

Preheat oven to 375 degrees.
1. Pour the oil into a heavy pot, heat, and add the rice. Stir the rice over medium heat until the grains turn from translucent to opaque white. Immediately pour in the grapefruit juice and chicken broth and season with salt and pepper.
2. Bring the liquid to a boil, cover pot, and place in the oven for 20 minutes. Remove from the oven and put aside for 5 minutes, still covered. Then scrape the rice into a mixing bowl, fluff with a fork, and stir in the yogurt.

NOTE: The rice can also be cooked on the stove top by reducing the flame to its lowest point and placing a heat-deflector pad under the covered pot.

MARINATED ZUCCHINI

Buy baby zucchini, if available. The taste will be the same, but smaller slices make a prettier garnish.

Makes about 3 cups

1 pound zucchini
3 tablespoons sugar
½ cup lime juice (3 or 4 limes)
1 sprig fresh basil or 1 tablespoon dried

1. Slice the zucchini into thin rounds and place them in a mixing bowl. There should be about 4 cups. Sprinkle on the

sugar and pour in the lime juice. Turn the slices with your hands to coat them evenly with the sugar and juice. If using fresh basil, break the sprig in half and tuck both pieces into the bowl. If using dried basil, simply sprinkle it in and mix the zucchini again.

2. Cover and put aside to marinate at room temperature for at least 4 hours, mixing occasionally. Refrigerate until needed. (This keeps very well in the refrigerator for 3 or 4 days. It is best to stir it every other day.) To serve, drain off the juice and remove the basil sprigs.

ORANGE COLE SLAW

A hand-held grater is necessary to achieve the proper texture of the carrots and orange, both of which must be reduced to fine bits. The cabbage, on the other hand, can be shredded in a food processor or with a knife. The orange is not visible, which adds a note of surprise to the first pleasurable taste.

Makes 2¹/₂ quarts

> ¹/₂ cabbage (about 1¹/₂ pounds)
> 4 carrots
> 1 seedless orange
> 2 tablespoons coarse salt
> 1¹/₄ to 1¹/₂ cups mayonnaise

1. Cut the cabbage into wedges, remove the core. Shred in a food processor or with a knife cut across each wedge to produce slices between ¹/₈ and ¹/₄ inch thick. Separate the cabbage shreds and place in a large mixing bowl.

2. Grate the orange rind directly into the bowl of cabbage, being careful not to include any of the white pith. With a knife cut away and discard all the bitter pith, then grate the orange into the bowl, followed by the carrots. Sprinkle with salt, toss all together, and let stand for 15 minutes.

3. Add 1¹/₄ cups mayonnaise and mix well. If you prefer a

moister slaw, add the remaining ¼ cup mayonnaise and mix again.

ITALIAN GREEN BEAN SALAD

Lettuce salads present a problem on a buffet table as they go limp from contact with the dressing after standing. Vegetable salads present no such problem, especially this slightly Italianate one.

Serves 6

½ cup olive oil
1 cup chopped onions
2 pounds fresh green beans
1 cup peeled, chopped tomatoes
1½ teaspoons salt
½ teaspoon pepper
1 teaspoon basil
½ teaspoon oregano
lemon wedges

1. Heat the oil in a saucepan and add the onions. Sauté the onions, covered, for about 10 minutes; do not allow them to brown. Add the beans, cover, and cook over low heat for 10 minutes, stirring occasionally. Add the tomatoes, salt, pepper, basil, and oregano, then cover and simmer for another 10 to 15 minutes or just until the beans are crisp-tender; do not allow them to become completely soft. Cool. If prepared in advance, refrigerate the beans, but bring back to room temperature before serving.

2. To serve, pile the salad on a platter and surround with the lemon wedges.

SOUFFLÉ GLACÉ AUX FRAISES
(FROZEN STRAWBERRY SOUFFLÉ)

Both hot and frozen soufflés are dramatic presentations, but while the former causes anxiety fits, the latter patiently waits in the freezer. A rich and luscious dessert, Frozen Strawberry Soufflé should be made when the berries are at their juiciest. This large soufflé is a stunning finale to a buffet dinner.

Serves 14

2½ cups sugar
¾ cup water
1 quart strawberries
1 tablespoon orange liqueur
1 tablespoon lemon juice
10 eggs
2 cups whipping cream
few drops red food color (optional)
Raspberry Sauce (page 250) (optional)
Garnish: whipped cream and strawberries

1. Boil the sugar and water together until they form a light syrup (220 degrees on a candy thermometer). Put the syrup aside to cool. Select a 12-cup soufflé mold and fit an aluminum foil collar around it. Chill a bowl for whipping the cream.
2. Rinse and hull the berries and place them in a blender or food processor. Add the orange liqueur and lemon juice and puree. There should be at least 2 cups of puree. Strain to remove the seeds.
3. Separate the eggs, putting all the yolks in a large mixing bowl and 4 of the whites in another bowl; reserve the remaining 6 whites for another use. Beat the yolks with an electric beater while pouring most of the sugar syrup over them; reserve about ¾ cup of the syrup in the pot. Suspend the bowl over a pot of barely simmering water and beat the yolks until they turn a light, frothy yellow, then turn very, very pale. The

volume of the mixture should at least double and the sauce should form a ribbon. Maintain a low heat at all times or there is a risk of the eggs cooking into hard curds. Remove the bowl from the heat and beat for another minute. Pour the strawberry puree over the sauce while beating. Add the red food color if desired and beat to blend in well. Put the strawberry sauce aside to cool.

4. Slowly reheat the reserved syrup in the pot while beating the 4 egg whites to soft peaks. Increase the heat under the syrup and bring it to the bubbling stage. Pour the hot syrup over the whites while beating at high speed. Continue beating to cool the whites. They should be thick and dense.

5. When the whites are completely cool, whip the cream. (If you have only 1 set of beaters, first rinse them well and put them, still wet, in the freezer for 5 minutes.) Using the chilled bowl and chilled beaters, beat the cream until very firm, then lightly fold it, a third at a time, into the beaten egg whites. Fold the egg white-cream combination into the strawberry sauce, a third at a time, working very lightly so as not to break down the volume. Pour the soufflé mixture into the prepared soufflé dish and freeze for at least 6 hours.

6. Remove the soufflé from the freezer at least ½ hour before serving. Decorate with strawberries and whipped cream. Pass the raspberry sauce, if desired.

Picnics and Barbecues

Picnic food can be anything you want to make it; I've even used refrigerator leftovers. For those who picnic in the backyard, anything goes. If there are grills, then meat, fish, and even vegetables can be cooked. If you walk deep into the woods or to an isolated beach, a hamper of cold delights is in order. To be really successful, however, the food must assert itself. Delicate flavors and aromas are lost when competing with the green smell of the outdoors, animated conversation, fun and games, and smoky grills, not to mention neighbors who bring along insect sprays. The following recipes are meant to hold their own in the face of such competition.

DEVILED CHICKEN

After chicken is treated to a bread coating it becomes perfect finger food, ideal for picnics. In this recipe a sharp mustard coating hides under the bread crumbs and gives the poultry an entirely new character. The quality of the mustard is important: if real Dijon mustard isn't used, it should at least be a Dijon-type.

Serves 8

8 large pieces of chicken, breasts or legs
½ cup oil
6 tablespoons strong Dijon mustard
3 tablespoons finely minced shallots
½ teaspoon dried tarragon
½ teaspoon dried thyme
⅛ teaspoon Tabasco
1 teaspoon Worcestershire sauce
3 to 4 cups bread crumbs

1. Preheat broiler to moderately hot. Place the chicken pieces on the broiling rack, skin side down, and sprinkle oil over each piece. Place the rack under the broiler about 5 inches away from the heat and broil for 5 minutes. Sprinkle with oil again and broil for another 5 minutes. Turn the chicken pieces and repeat the process on the other side. Remove from the oven.

2. Meanwhile, blend together the mustard, shallots, tarragon, thyme, Tabasco, and Worcestershire sauce. Remove about ½ cup of the oil drippings from the broiling pan and beat into the mustard mixture. Reserve the rest of the oil drippings.

3. Put the bread crumbs in a large dish. Then use a pastry brush to paint each piece of chicken very thoroughly with the mustard mixture. Put the chicken pieces in the bread-crumb dish and carefully pat a thick coating of crumbs over the entire

surface. Return the chicken pieces to the broiling rack, again skin side down, and allow to dry for at least 30 minutes.

4. Dribble half the reserved drippings over the chicken pieces, place in the broiler about 6 to 7 inches from the flame, and broil for 5 minutes. Dribble on some fresh oil and broil for 5 more minutes. Turn pieces over and repeat the process for the other side, using all the drippings you have saved. The chicken is done when the drumstick is tender to the touch or when juices run clear yellow when the meat is pierced with a fork. Do not overcook the chicken, or the meat tends to dry out.

CHICKEN IN BEER

Only the cook need know what cooking liquid is used in this recipe. It is not a beery flavor that comes through, but one that brings back memories of farm-fresh chicken. Another advantage—chickens that are a bit tough with age on them are tenderized during the baking. It is delicious hot at home or cold in the picnic basket. Try it both ways.

Serves 4

4 tablespoons butter
3 to 3½ pounds chicken pieces
salt and pepper
3 cups beer (approximately)

Preheat oven to 375 degrees.

1. Select a baking dish that will hold the chicken in one layer. Grease the dish with about 1 tablespoon of butter. Salt and pepper both sides of the chicken pieces and place them in the dish.

2. Cut the remaining butter into small pieces and scatter over the chicken. Pour in just enough beer to almost cover the chicken, pouring against the side of the dish so as not to

disturb the butter or seasonings. Bake, uncovered, for about 45 minutes, basting occasionally. When serving hot, spoon a few tablespoons of the beer over each portion.

PARSLEY-STUFFED CORNISH GAME HENS

This recipe fits into several menu sections in this book. Served hot at dinner, the Cornish game hens make succulent eating. Served cold, they brighten any luncheon menu or buffet table. But I decided to place the recipe in this picnic chapter simply to encourage its use as a refreshing change of pace from the usual outdoor fare.

Serves 4

Stuffing:
3 tablespoons butter
1 medium onion, chopped
2 cups parsley leaves, lightly packed
juice of ½ lemon
salt and pepper
1 slice white bread
2 Cornish game hens
2 tablespoons butter
salt and pepper
¼ to ½ cup chicken broth

1. In a skillet, melt 1 tablespoon of butter. Stir in the onions, cover, and simmer over medium heat for 5 minutes. Meanwhile, roughly chop the parsley. Add it to the onions with the remaining 2 tablespoons of butter. Sprinkle with the lemon juice, salt, and pepper. Remove the skillet from the heat and rub the bread between your hands to crumble it into the skillet. Stir all the ingredients together.

2. Stuff the two birds and truss securely. Melt 2 tablespoons

butter in a deep casserole that will just hold the game hens. (If the pot is too large, the butter will burn; if too small, the skin of the birds will be damaged when turning.) When the butter is hot, add the birds, breast side down, then brown on all sides, turning them with two wooden spoons so as not to break the skin. Salt and pepper them as you turn.

3. Position the birds breast side up and add ¼ cup chicken broth. Baste the birds, place a sheet of aluminum foil over them, then cover with a lid. Cook over low heat for about 30 minutes, basting several times. Add a little more chicken broth if necessary to keep the liquid at about ¼ inch level. Test for doneness by wiggling one leg of hen, which should feel quite loose, or by piercing the skin in the upper thigh; if the juices run clear, the bird is thoroughly cooked. I prefer to stop the cooking when there is still a trace of pink in the juices.

4. If you would like to crisp the breast skin, place the pot under a preheated broiler for a minute or two. Let the game hens stand for 10 minutes, remove the string, and cut in half.

CHINESE CHICKEN SALAD

Since no mayonnaise is used in the dressing, this is an ideal salad to pack into the picnic basket, no matter how hot the day. A few chopped walnuts can be tossed in, if you like.

Serves 8

3 whole chicken breasts, poached
½ pound thinly sliced boiled ham
½ pound bean sprouts
salt and pepper
¾ cup oil
¼ cup soy sauce
2 tablespoons bourbon or whiskey
lettuce

167

1. Remove all skin and bones from the chickens and use a very sharp knife to cut the meat into long julienne strips of matchstick thickness. Cut the boiled ham into strips of the same size and combine the two meats in a mixing bowl. Add the bean sprouts and sprinkle lightly with salt and pepper.

2. Prepare the dressing by beating together the oil, soy sauce, bourbon, salt, and pepper. Pour the dressing over the meats and sprouts and toss well. Serve on lettuce leaves.

"GAMY" TURKEY DRUMSTICKS

Chicken legs as picnic or barbecue fare hold no surprises, but turkey drumsticks are another matter. The marinade used on these fleshy pieces imparts the deep flavor of game. As good as these drumsticks are, the numerous tendons in the meat mark them for informal family dinners at home, the picnic basket, or even the barbecue grill.

Serves 4

4 1-pound turkey drumsticks
1½ tablespoons dried rosemary
2 garlic cloves
½ cup olive oil
3 tablespoons red wine vinegar
salt and pepper
½ cup white wine
1 teaspoon aromatic bitters

1. Rinse the drumsticks and dry them well. Place them in an enameled cast-iron pan or other nonreactive baking pan that can be put on the stove.

2. Chop the rosemary and garlic together and put them into a jar. Add the olive oil, red wine vinegar, salt, and pepper and shake well. Pour half of the marinade over the drumsticks and

turn them to ensure that all surfaces are coated, using your fingers to spread the marinade if necessary. Marinate for at least 3 hours, or overnight in the refrigerator.

Preheat oven to 450 degrees.

3. Turn the drumsticks and bake in their pan for 10 minutes. Use tongs to turn them over and bake another 10 minutes to brown other side.

4. Reduce the heat to 350 degrees. Turn the drumsticks one-quarter of the way so that the unbrowned edges are uppermost, spoon over them half the remaining marinade, and bake for 15 minutes. Turn other unbrowned edge up, pour on the rest of the marinade, and bake for a final 15 minutes.

5. Remove the drumsticks from the baking dish. Pour the baking liquid into a bowl, spoon off the fat that rises to the top, and return the juices to the pan. Add the white wine and bitters and place the pan on the stove over moderately high heat. While the liquid boils, scrape the bottom with a wooden spatula to loosen the coagulated juices.

6. If serving "Gamy" Turkey Drumsticks as a hot dish at home, simply pour the sauce into a warm bowl and pass it at the table. For a picnic, pour the sauce into a jar and use it for dipping pieces of the tasty meat. If you're barbecuing the drumsticks, the sauce must be sacrificed. Grilling time is about 1 hour.

TURKEY DRUMSTICK BAKE

Here is a recipe that lets you carry two foods in one dish: the drumsticks and a stuffing. One can mix the stuffing in a bowl, then transfer to the baking dish, but why? There is less cleanup this way. Extra vegetables can be added to the stuffing, such as sliced celery, mushrooms, or even corn.

Serves 4

½ cup butter
1 cup chopped onion
10 slices stale bread
1 teaspoon celery salt
½ teaspoon thyme
½ teaspoon sage
salt and pepper
½ cup chopped parsley
1 cup liquid, either milk or cooking juices from
   mushrooms or beans
2 to 3 tablespoons oil
4 turkey drumsticks

Preheat oven to 375 degrees.

1. Melt 2 tablespoons butter in a small pan. Add the onions, cover, and simmer gently without browning for about 10 minutes.

2. Meanwhile select a deep baking dish that will hold the drumsticks, and break the bread into small pieces directly into the dish. Add the cooked onion, all the spices, and the parsley and toss mixture with your hands. Melt 2 tablespoons of butter in the pan used for the onions and pour it over the bread. Pour in the cup of liquid, toss again, and pat the stuffing into a smooth layer.

3. Rub oil over the drumsticks and sprinkle them with salt and pepper. Lay the drumsticks on the stuffing and place dish in the oven. Melt the remaining 4 tablespoons of butter and

brush over the drumsticks while occasionally turning them. The turkey should be cooked in about 1 to 1¼ hours. To test for doneness, pierce the fleshy part of the leg with a small sharp knife; if the juices run clear or pale rose, the meat is done. Serve hot or at room temperature.

GRILLED FLANK STEAK

This lean morsel of beef is given many names—Plank Steak, London Broil, Jiffy Steak, and even grandiose Flank Steak Fillet. No matter what the name, it is very tasty meat that responds to the easiest grilling treatment or to stuffing and braising. I like it almost more as a cold leftover, especially when given an extra flavor boost with this marinade. It is ideal for outdoor barbecues since it grills so quickly.

Serves 6

1 2-pound flank steak
2 tablespoons oil
1 teaspoon sage
1 teaspoon rosemary
1 tablespoon lemon juice
¼ cup whiskey (straight or blended)
1 garlic clove

1. Place the flank steak in a baking dish and rub it all over with the oil. Crush the sage and rosemary in the palm of your hand, then rub the herbs on both sides of the meat. Sprinkle the lemon juice and whiskey on both sides as well. Cut the garlic clove into thin slivers, rub a few of the pieces over the meat, then distribute them over both surfaces of the meat. Put the steak aside to marinate at least 1 hour, preferably 2. Turn the meat several times while marinating.

2. Preheat an outdoor grill, cast-iron grill, or a heavy skillet. With a thick wad of paper toweling, smear oil over the hot grill. Lightly dry the surface of the meat with paper towels, and

remove the garlic slices if you wish. Cook the steak on the hot grill for about 2 minutes, brush with the marinade, and turn over to grill the second side. Reduce the heat to medium, or move the grill farther away from the fire bed. If more marinade remains in the dish, brush the other side as well. Sprinkle with salt and pepper. Cook no more than a minute or two on the second side, just until the back of a fork feels some resistance when pressed against the meat. The meat will be medium-rare.

3. Remove the meat to a carving board and let stand for a few minutes. Cut across the grain at an angle to produce long, thin strips; the meat *must* be cut thin. Serve on warm plates.

BEEF SALAD

Beef Salad is usually prepared from leftover roasts or braised meats, and very good eating it is. But when a larger quantity is needed, the meat has to be specially prepared, and this is the way I like to do it. The beef brisket is first marinated, then braised, and emerges moist and full of flavor—a treat in any hamper.

Serves 8

3 pounds beef brisket

Marinade:
   salt and pepper
   2 cups red wine
   1/4 cup brandy
   1 large onion, cut into thick slices
   2 carrots, cut into thick slices
   1 celery rib, broken into 2 or 3 pieces
   5 or 6 unpeeled garlic cloves, mashed
   1/2 teaspoon thyme
   1/2 teaspoon sage
   1/2 teaspoon allspice
   1 cup beef broth

2 pounds potatoes, cooked in their skins
½ green pepper, chopped
2 tablespoons capers

Dressing:
   1 cup oil
   2 teaspoons prepared mustard
   2 tablespoons vinegar
   ¼ cup lemon juice
   2 tablespoons minced shallots
   ½ teaspoon celery seed
   ¾ teaspoon thyme
   ½ teaspoon tarragon
   ½ teaspoon basil
   1 tablespoon minced parsley
   salt and pepper

lettuce
tomato wedges
4 hard-boiled eggs, cut into quarters

1. Place the beef in a glass dish or enameled cast-iron pot and add all the marinade ingredients except the beef broth. Marinate the meat for at least 4 hours and preferably overnight, turning occasionally.

2. Add the beef broth to the pot, place on a low flame, and bring the liquid to a simmer. Cover and cook gently for 1½ to 2 hours or until tender. Cool, cover, and refrigerate.

3. When ready to prepare the salad, lift the beef from its cooking stock, trim away all visible fat, cut into thin slices, and place in a deep mixing bowl. Peel the potatoes, cut them into 1¼-inch slices, and add to the meat along with the green pepper and capers.

4. Shake all ingredients for the dressing in a covered jar and pour over the salad. Use your hands to carefully mix the salad; do not break the potato slices. Let stand at least 1 hour, then cover and refrigerate.

5. If serving the Beef Salad at home, bring it back to almost room temperature. Line a large platter with lettuce, mound the

salad in the center, and garnish with the tomato and hard-boiled-egg wedges. To take along on a picnic, keep refrigerated until packing the hamper and garnish at serving time.

MARINATED SIRLOIN STEAK

If this tasty meat salad is prepared shortly before leaving for the picnic, it will be perfect when you are ready to eat. It should marinate for at least half an hour but only improves if given more time. A word of caution: don't overcook the steak when grilling it; much of its success depends on tender, rosy strips of meat.

Serves 6

2½ pounds boneless sirloin steak, grilled to medium-rare
    and cooled
1 large Bermuda onion, thinly sliced
1½ cups sour cream
juice of 1½ lemons
1 tablespoon mustard
salt and pepper
Garnish: lettuce, chopped parsley, tomato wedges

1. Trim all fat off the meat and cut meat into very thin slices. Place the slices in a bowl with the onion.
2. Stir together the sour cream, lemon juice, mustard, salt, and pepper and pour this marinade over the meat and onions. Mix very well, using your hands to coat the meat. Let stand at least half an hour.
3. Line the platter or individual plate with the lettuce and mound the marinated meat in the center. Sprinkle with chopped parsley and garnish with tomato wedges.

BARBECUED SPARERIBS

Sparerib eating is messy eating and therefore ideally suited for the outdoor barbecue. Though the ribs can be plunked on the grill with no prior preparation, I find that boiling them for 5 minutes drives off excess fat and softens the flesh, making tastier eating. No recipe is included for barbecue sauce because everyone has his own favorite mix or brand. Mine comes out of a bottle.

1 pound spareribs per person (at least)
barbecue sauce

1. Trim off excess fat from the spareribs and boil in a large quantity of water for 5 minutes. Discard the water.

2. Prepare the fire in the firebox. When the ashes are gray, place the ribs on the grill positioned about 8 inches above the fire. Spareribs are better if cooked slowly. Grill for about 20 minutes, then turn and grill the other side for 20 minutes.

3. Turn again and, with a long-handled brush, paint the ribs with the barbecue sauce. Keep painting and turning the ribs at 10-minute intervals until the ribs have cooked for 1 hour in all. To check for doneness, pierce the meat with a small sharp knife; if the juices run clear the ribs are cooked. Cut into strips and serve accompanied by lots of paper napkins.

TAMALE PIE

When planning a picnic menu, keep in mind that you are better off carrying as few dishes as possible. Here in one tasty package you have a starch, the emphatically seasoned meat, and even a vegetable. To gild the whole affair, cheese is strewn over the top.

Serves 6

Pie Shell:
1 cup yellow cornmeal
2 cups water
1 teaspoon salt
1 teaspoon ground cumin
1 tablespoon butter

Filling:
¼ cup oil
1 medium onion, chopped (about ¾ cup)
1 pound ground beef
½ green pepper, chopped (about ½ cup)
1 teaspoon minced garlic
1 tablespoon flour
1 1-pound can tomatoes
1 1-pound can corn kernels, vacuum packed or drained
1 teaspoon ground cumin
2 teaspoons Worcestershire sauce
½ teaspoon chili powder
1 teaspoon salt
¼ pound sharp cheddar cheese, grated

1. To make the pie shell, in a pot stir together the cornmeal, water, salt, and cumin. Cook until thick, about 3 or 4 minutes after the water begins to boil.

2. Meanwhile, liberally grease a 1½-quart shallow casserole or deep pie dish with the tablespoon of butter. Scoop the cornmeal mush into the dish, grease your fingertips with butter, and pat the mush into a thick shell against the sides of the dish. Do not extend the mush into a decorative rim above the dish, since it will dry out during the baking. Refrigerate to firm the shell.

Preheat oven to 350 degrees.

3. To make the filling, heat the oil in a skillet, add the onion, and cook for about a minute while stirring. Add the ground meat, turn up the heat, and cook for about 3 minutes, stirring so that all of the beef is fried. Add the green pepper and garlic and sprinkle in the flour. Stir to evenly distribute the flour and cook for a minute. Add the tomatoes, crushing the pulp with

your hands as you add them to the skillet. Then add the corn kernels, cumin, Worcestershire sauce, chili powder, and salt. Stir and cook, uncovered, for 5 minutes.

4. Spoon the filling into the prepared cornmeal shell and bake for 30 minutes. Sprinkle the grated cheese over the top and bake for 10 minutes more or until the cheese melts. Cut into wedges and serve.

MEAT PIE

This is not the kind of pie you expect; in a way, it more closely resembles a cobbler. The filling is not baked in a pie shell but within the batter itself. Although the pie looks its best when hot and puffy right out of the oven, its hearty flavor at room temperature makes it excellent picnic eating, too.

Serves 6

1 large tomato
¾ pound Polish sausage or leftover tongue or ham
1½ cups milk
1 egg
salt and pepper
1 teaspoon dry mustard
1 teaspoon Worcestershire sauce
1 cup flour

Preheat oven to 375 degrees.

1. Slice the tomato and arrange in a layer in a 9-inch pie dish. Slice the sausage and scatter over the tomato.

2. In the jar of a blender process thoroughly the milk, egg, salt, pepper, dry mustard, and Worcestershire sauce. Add the flour and process again very briefly, just enough to incorporate the flour.

3. Pour the batter over the tomatoes and meat and bake for about 45 minutes or until the top is brown and puffy.

ORIENTAL PORK KEBABS

Cooking over coals figures prominently in many Oriential cuisines, so it seemed logical to borrow some of their flavorings for these kebabs.

Serves 6

2½ pounds pork loin, cut into 1-inch cubes
1 medium onion, finely chopped (about 1 cup)
2 teaspoons ground coriander
2 teaspoons cumin
½ teaspoon ground ginger
2 teaspoons soy sauce
¼ cup lemon juice
2 tablespoons sherry
2 teaspoons oil
24 mushroom caps

1. In a mixing bowl combine all the ingredients except the mushroom caps. Mix well, cover, and let stand at room temperature for at least 3 hours, or overnight in the refrigerator. Turn the meat occasionally.
2. String skewers beginning with a mushroom cap, rounded side out, then 4 or 5 pieces of meat, and finally another mushroom cap, again rounded side out. There should be enough for 12 to 14 skewers.
3. Brush the kebabs lightly with the marinade and grill over medium-hot coals for 4 to 5 minutes. Turn the skewers, brush again with marinade, and grill for about 7 minutes. To test for doneness, with a small sharp knife pierce a piece of meat; if juices are rosy pink the meat is ready to eat, but for completely cooked pork wait until the juices run clear. Continue grilling to reach the desired degree of doneness, brushing intermittently with the marinade.

CHICK-PEA SALAD

This salad can be put together right out of a well-stocked cupboard. Cans of chick-peas and beets should always be kept on hand since they can be used so very many ways. Here they are mixed with red onion and celery, but regular yellow onion or scallions could replace the red onion, and zucchini or thin carrot strips might stand in for the celery.

Serves 4

1 1-pound can chick-peas, drained and rinsed
1 8-ounce can sliced or diced beets, drained
¼ cup thinly sliced red onion
½ cup diced celery
¼ cup olive oil
2 tablespoons wine vinegar
1 teaspoon prepared mustard
salt and pepper
lettuce

1. In a mixing bowl, combine the chick-peas, beets, red onion, and celery. In a jar, shake together the olive oil, vinegar, mustard, salt, and pepper.
2. Pour the dressing over the salad ingredients. Mix well, preferably with your hands so the chick-peas will not be mashed. Spoon onto lettuce leaves, either in a serving bowl or on individual plates.

ROASTED GREEN PEPPERS

Here is a perfect side dish to accompany barbecued meats. To economize on energy, pop the peppers into the oven when baking other food. The oven temperature can vary since the limp condition of the peppers will let you know when they are done.

Serves 8

8 green peppers
juice of 2 lemons
¼ cup olive oil
1 teaspoon oregano
salt and pepper

Preheat oven to 375 degrees.

1. Rinse the peppers, place on a baking sheet, and bake for 20 to 25 minutes. The peppers will be soft and limp when they are cooked through. Let cool.

2. Cut the peppers in half lengthwise, scoop out and discard the seeds, and place peppers in a bowl. Beat together the lemon juice, olive oil, oregano, salt, and pepper and pour over the peppers. Toss the peppers with your hands to coat all surfaces with the dressing.

APPLE-CHEESE BAKE

Dessert and a cheese course are baked together in this dish. It could even be served along with meats and poultry if you omit the nuts and reduce the amount of sugar.

Serves 6

6 medium apples
⅓ cup brown sugar, well packed
½ teaspoon salt
¾ teaspoon cinnamon
3 tablespoons orange juice
1 tablespoon brandy or whiskey

1 tablespoon lemon juice
¾ cup chopped nuts, preferably pecans
butter

Cheese Topping:
   ¾ cup flour
   ¼ cup brown sugar, well packed
   1 cup shredded cheddar cheese
   ¼ cup butter, melted

Preheat oven to 375 degrees.

1. Peel and core the apples, cut into thick slices, and put them in a large bowl. Sprinkle over the apples the ⅓ cup brown sugar, salt, cinnamon, orange juice, brandy, lemon juice, and nuts and mix thoroughly so that all apple slices are well coated. Butter a 2-quart baking dish and pat the apples into the dish, smoothing them into an even layer.

2. To make topping, in a small bowl mix together the flour, ¼ cup brown sugar, and cheese. Spread this topping over the apples and sprinkle with the melted butter.

3. Bake for about 45 minutes or until the apples are tender when pierced with a sharp knife. Apple-Cheese Bake is best served warm or at room temperature, but not piping hot.

PEANUT BUTTER CUPCAKES

These cupcakes are very good eating even without a topping, which makes them perfect for the picnic basket. For at-home consumption, gild them with Whipped Honey Frosting (page 252) or Cream Cheese Icing (pages 252–53).

Makes 12 cupcakes

½ cup peanut butter (4 ounces)
1¼ cups water
1½ cups flour
¾ cup sugar
1 teaspoon baking soda
1 teaspoon baking powder
½ teaspoon salt
½ cup oil
1 tablespoon vanilla
2 tablespoons vinegar (not wine vinegar)

Preheat oven to 375 degrees.

1. In a small pot heat together the peanut butter and water in order to dissolve the peanut butter; cool to lukewarm.

2. Measure into a mixing bowl the flour, sugar, baking soda, baking powder, and salt. Stir with a whisk to mix all the dry ingredients, then add the melted peanut butter, oil, and vanilla and whisk thoroughly. Add the vinegar and stir well to incorporate it completely into the batter.

3. Fill each compartment of a greased muffin tin about two-thirds full of batter. There should be enough for twelve muffins. Bake the muffins for about 20 minutes or until they puff a little and begin pulling away from the sides of the tin. A toothpick plunged in the center should come out dry.

NO-KNEAD DILL BREAD

At picnics and barbecues, plain breads are often upstaged by all the other aromas and forceful flavors and can end up being just filler food or sauce absorbers. That is why this easy-to-make bread is in this section—it has the perky smell of dill that holds its own in stronger company. Try toasting it on the grill for another treat.

Makes 1 8-inch round loaf

1 package active dry yeast (¼ ounce) or 1 cake compressed yeast (.6 ounce)
¼ cup warm water
1 cup small-curd cottage cheese
3 tablespoons butter
2 tablespoons honey
1 teaspoon dried onion soup
1 tablespoon chopped fresh dill or 2 teaspoons dried dill weed
¼ teaspoon baking soda
1 teaspoon salt
1 beaten egg
2¼ to 2½ cups flour

1. In a large mixing bowl, soften the yeast in the warm water; stir to dissolve the yeast.

2. In a saucepan, heat the cottage cheese, 1 tablespoon butter, and the honey until they are lukewarm. Add the dried onion soup, dill, baking soda, salt, and the egg. Stir to blend all the flavorings.

3. Scrape the cottage cheese mixture into the yeast and water and stir. Add enough flour to make a firm ball of dough; stir it with a wooden spoon but do not knead. Soak a cloth with hot water, wring it out, and place it over the mixing bowl. Let the dough rise in a warm place until it has doubled in bulk, about 1 hour.

4. Stir down the dough. Use 1 tablespoon of butter to grease an 8-inch round cake pan and put the dough in the pan, patting to smooth it a little. Let it rise for about 45 minutes.

Preheat oven to 350 degrees.

5. Place the baking pan in the oven and bake for 40 to 50 minutes or until the top is nicely browned. Cool the bread slightly, then remove it to a rack. To achieve a shiny crust, melt the remaining tablespoon of butter and brush it over the top.

Dinner Parties

"Company" menus have changed a lot in the last decade. Dinner parties used to call for your best bib-and-tucker recipes, which were usually expensive, laboriously produced, and predictable. The times, the economy, and food habits have changed. Today, hearty cassoulet, stews, pasta, choucroute garnie, and homemade pâtés show up as often as roast beef or sautéed chicken. One famous New York hostess even invited guests for a black-tie dinner and served boiled beef and vegetables. The guests all thought it very chic. It all comes down to how the food is presented and the ambience surrounding it.

Within this chapter the reader will find a number of easy-to-prepare dishes that have an element of novelty about them. Instead of shrimp cocktail, try Mussel Cocktail. Follow creamy Chestnut Soup with Turkey Breast with Oyster Sauce, Duck with Grapefruit, or perhaps Scallop Brochettes. Vegetables need not be a letdown, not with the likes of Gingered Carrots, Baked Bean Sprouts, Parsley Fritters, or Cauliflower with Caper-Butter Sauce. The dessert recipes bring the meal to a close on a soft, soothing note. However, the most surprising dessert of all is not printed here, simply because it requires no cooking: fill small glasses with icy-cold French Sauternes to sip accompanied by thin cookies.

Once you've carefully selected your menu, don't sabotage it by serving heavy hors d'oeuvres. Any cocktail-hour snacks should be light and limited in number. Do not prolong the cocktail hour unnecessarily; forty-five minutes is enough time for even latecomers to have a short drink. One should not delay the dinner for everyone if one couple arrives unconscionably late; simply mention that there will be wine at the table. If the drinking time is unreasonably extended, guests may not make it to the table with clear heads and undulled palates.

To ensure good dinner-table conversation, the seating should be as carefully planned as the menu. Beyond the guests of honor, who always sit to the right of the host and hostess, there are no set rules, except in situations calling for diplomatic protocol. The hostess must be sensitive to the personalities of the guests and attempt to match people of similar interests or simply those who might enjoy each other's company. Be careful of placing two single people together, lest they think you are matchmaking.

Most single hosts or hostesses and couples work out their own styles of serving without help. Often the dinner plates and food platters are placed on a sideboard; then the hostess prepares the plates and the host serves. Another method is to have the guests help themselves from the sideboard before sitting down, but the host or hostess should offer seconds, thus avoiding disrupting the entire table. As mentioned before, a tea cart to hold clean and dirty dishes can be a great aid.

All flatware is arranged in the order of use, working from the outside in, with forks on the left and knives and spoons on the right. An oyster or shrimp fork is the one exception—it is always placed on the right. The butter knife is placed across the top of the bread-and-butter plate, which sits above the forks. Dessert forks and spoons are either laid horizontally above the dinner plate or presented on the dessert plate. Glassware is set from right to left, beginning with the white wine glass above the knives, then the red wine glass, and finally the water glass. *If it is a festive occasion and champagne is being poured with dessert, place the champagne glass above the red wine glass. It takes a large table to hold a complete set of glasses, so you may want to bring in the champagne glasses after removing the red and white wine glasses. Before dessert, all service pieces used during the meal should be taken away, including the salt and pepper shakers.*

When serving help is engaged, they should present platters or completed plates from the left, remove dishes from the right, and pour wine from the right. They also crumb the table before dessert is brought in.

When the fruits of all your work and planning are brought before the gathering of friends and family, survey it all with a feeling of pride, pleasure, and gratitude. This is the moment to contemplate saying grace before the meal begins, in whatever fashion you chose.

CHESTNUT SOUP

Everyone has his favorite way of getting rid of chestnut shells. Methods of shelling include pan-roasting, pan-frying, deep-frying, and boiling. In each case you start by making crosswise gashes in the flat side of each.

I have found that the simplest way is boiling the chestnuts for 2 minutes, then lifting a few at a time out of the water and pulling off the thick outer skin, along with (one hopes) the thin inner one. Any stubborn ones can be tossed back into the hot water. They must be warm for easy peeling, so if you're preparing a large quantity, it might be a good idea to reheat the water during the operation.

Serves 8

4 tablespoons butter
¼ cup chopped onion
2 celery stalks, coarsely chopped
1 pound raw chestnuts, peeled
1 quart strong chicken broth
salt and pepper
1 to 1½ cups light cream
3 tablespoons butter (optional)
croutons for garnish

1. Melt the 4 tablespoons butter in a small skillet, add the onion and celery, cover, and simmer gently for 5 minutes. Stir once or twice. Meanwhile, put the peeled chestnuts in a nonreactive pot and add the chicken broth, then scrape in the cooked onions and celery. Add salt (use very little if using canned broth) and pepper. Cover and bring to a boil, then reduce heat and simmer for 30 minutes or until the chestnuts are soft when pierced with a small sharp knife.

2. Cool slightly, then ladle the soup into a blender or food processor and puree until smooth. Pour the puree back into the pot and stir in enough cream to reach the consistency you

want. Reheat slowly and taste for seasonings; correct if necessary.

3. For a richer soup, just before serving add the extra 3 tablespoons of butter and stir until it melts. (Omit this butter addition if serving cold.) Sprinkle a few croutons on top for a touch of color.

QUICK SEAFOOD BISQUE

Here is an ace in the hole for last-minute cooking. It is based on several cans from your emergency shelf, but if you don't tell, no one will ever guess.

Serves 8

1 can condensed cream of tomato soup
1 can condensed pea soup
2 cups clam juice
1 cup heavy cream
milk (optional)
salt and pepper
few drops of Tabasco
1 tablespoon dry sherry
1 teaspoon brandy
shrimp for garnish, preferably fresh

1. In a pot, combine the 2 soups and slowly stir in the clam juice and cream. This should be a fairly thick mixture; if you prefer a thinner bisque, add some milk. Season with salt, pepper, and Tabasco.

2. Heat the mixture slowly, stirring occasionally. When the bisque is really hot, add the sherry and brandy, bring to the boiling point, and remove from heat.

3. Pour the bisque into individual soup bowls and garnish each one with a few small shrimp; if the shrimp are large, cut them into several pieces.

OYSTERS POLONAISE

Anytime you see the word "Polonaise" in a recipe title, look
for hard-boiled eggs somewhere. You'll find them here right on
top of the oysters as part of a seasoned coating. The oysters
are briefly warmed in the oven, which gives the delicate
morsels quite another character.

Serves 4

2 hard-boiled eggs, finely chopped
¼ cup parsley, finely chopped
1 teaspoon celery seed
salt and pepper
16 oysters on the half-shell
coarse salt (see note for Oysters à l'Escargot, pages 137–38)
   (optional)
⅓ cup butter
¼ cup bread crumbs
lemon wedges

Preheat oven to 350 degrees.

1. In a bowl mix together the eggs, parsley, celery seed,
salt, and pepper. Place the oysters in a jelly roll pan, preferably
on a salt bed. Cover each oyster with the seasoned egg
mixture. Bake for 5 or 6 minutes; oysters should be very
warm, but not quite hot.

2. Meanwhile, melt the butter in a small skillet and stir in
the crumbs. Cook slowly until the crumbs brown a little. Just
before serving oysters, spoon a teaspoonful of the crumbs over
each oyster. Serve with lemon wedges.

MOULES MARINÈRE (STEAMED MUSSELS)

You don't have to be French, Italian, or Spanish to enjoy mussels. It helps, though, since the cuisines of those countries make abundant use of these bivalves. Cleaning the crusty creatures takes a bit of patience, but it is simple work—and keep in mind what thrifty eating they are.

Serves 4 to 6

2 cups water
1 large onion, finely chopped
large herb bouquet (8 parsley sprigs, 1 large bay leaf, and
    tops of 2 celery ribs, all bundled and tied together)
½ teaspoon thyme
1 tablespoon juniper berries (optional, but recommended)
½ teaspoon salt
¼ teaspoon pepper
1 carrot, finely diced
¼ cup butter (optional)
½ lemon
5 pounds mussels
1 ½ cups dry white wine
¼ cup chopped parsley

1. In a large pot combine the water, onion, herb bouquet, thyme, juniper berries, salt, pepper, carrot, butter (if desired), and lemon, first squeezing the lemon juice into the water and then dropping in the lemon shell as well. Cover and bring to a boil, then simmer for 15 minutes. (This can be done early and the pot set aside for the final few minutes of cooking.)

2. Scrub the mussels with a stiff brush, then use a sharp knife to pull off the clinging beards (byssuses). Plunge the mussels into a large bowl of cold water, rough them up with your hands and drain immediately. The water should be rather clean at this point; if it's not, repeat process. Rinse one more time under cold running water. Be suspicious of any mussels

that seem exceptionally heavy—they could be full of sand rather than meat. A sure test is to push the halves of the shell against each other horizontally; if the mussel is sand-filled, the halves will slide apart. There will always be some mussels with shells that are partially open. Pinch them together; if they close up, they are fine, but if they remain stubbornly wide open, throw them away because they may be spoiled.

3. Pour the white wine into the simmering broth and bring it back to a full boil. Dump in the mussels and cover tightly. Keep on high heat and shake the pot once or twice during cooking to mix up the mussels. (If the pot is too large to shake easily, just stir quickly with a large spoon.) As soon as the mussels have opened, which should not take more than 5 minutes, they are ready.

4. Ladle the mussels into deep soup bowls and strain the broth over them, but do not pour from the very bottom of the pot since there is likely to be some sand there. Sprinkle with chopped parsley.

MUSSEL COCKTAIL

Even before shrimp prices attained celestial heights, I always preferred serving mussel cocktail as the opening course at dinner. The reasons make more sense than ever: it's inexpensive, it is an unexpected presentation, and you know you are working with a fresh product since mussels cannot be frozen.

Serves 6 to 8

3 quarts mussels, steamed (pages 191–92)
1/4 cup olive oil
1/4 cup dry white vermouth
juice of 1/2 lemon
1/4 teaspoon celery salt
salt and pepper
3/4 cup mayonnaise, preferably homemade

¼ cup chopped parsley
lettuce

1. While the mussels are steaming prepare the sauce in a mixing bowl. Whisk together the olive oil, vermouth, lemon juice, celery salt, salt, and pepper.

2. As soon as you can handle the mussels, remove the shells and drop the mussels into the dressing. When all the mussels have been shelled, toss them with the dressing; use your hands so as not to damage the delicate mussels. Cover and let stand at room temperature for at least 1 hour, stirring occasionally.

3. At serving time, drain the mussels from the marinade and beat enough of the marinade liquid into the mayonnaise to make a thin sauce. Fold the sauce into the mussels and add the chopped parsley. Heap the mussels into individual lettuce-lined bowls.

NOTE: For this recipe, the mussels can be cooked the day before serving, removed from their shells, and kept in the refrigerator in the strained cooking liquid. Drain off the liquid before proceeding with the recipe. Allow the mussels to stand at least 2 hours in the olive oil dressing.

MOULES FARCIES (STUFFED MUSSELS)

Bored with Clams Casino and Oysters Rockefeller? Try stuffed mussels and save a lot of money in the process.

Serves 6

½ cup butter, softened
1 cup very fine bread crumbs
2 tablespoons finely chopped shallots
1 tablespoon lemon juice
4 tablespoons finely chopped parsley
3 tablespoons brandy or bourbon
2 quarts mussels

1. Cream the butter in a deep bowl, then add all the other ingredients except the mussels.

2. Scrub and debeard the mussels (Steamed Mussels, pages 191–92). For the very best results the raw mussels should be opened with a blunt knife. (One can cheat and steam them open, but only barely. If overcooked at this point they will become rubbery when broiled.) Put the cleaned mussels in a covered pot without water or any other addition, and heat until they relax and begin to open. Remove one shell from each and leave the mussel on the other shell.

3. Spread stuffing on each mussel, making sure the meat is completely covered. Put under a hot broiler for 2 or 3 minutes or until the stuffing bubbles and is lightly browned.

SALMON IN CHAMPAGNE SAUCE

If you have a really fine champagne, save it to drink on a special occasion. However, reasonably priced champagnes or sparkling wines can be used successfully in the kitchen. Look for dry *(brut) vins mousseux* (bubbly wines) from France, Spain, or California. I am often asked whether white wine can't be substituted since the bubbles go off, anyway. It can, but I find that an indefinable spark separates the two. The late Dione Lucas used to make onion soup with champagne. To my frugal mind that seemed economic folly, and I tried making it with plain white wine instead. She was right.

Serves 8

Court Bouillon:
    1 quart water
    1 cup white wine
    1 medium carrot, sliced
    1 medium onion, sliced
    4 or 5 parsley sprigs
    ½ bay leaf

pinch of thyme
salt and pepper

2 tablespoons butter
3 shallots, minced
1 tablespoon flour
1½ cups champagne
1 cup heavy cream
8 salmon steaks

1. Combine all the ingredients for the court bouillon in a nonreactive pot, bring to a boil, partially cover, and simmer briskly for 20 minutes. Strain and cool.

2. In a heavy saucepan, heat the butter, add the shallots, cover, and simmer for 5 minutes or until the shallots are soft; do not allow them to brown. Add the flour and whisk until smooth; then, stirring constantly, slowly add the champagne. Remove from the heat and stir in the cream. Return the sauce to the heat and simmer over a very low flame for about 20 minutes or until reduced by a third. Cool.

Preheat oven to 375 degrees.

3. Place the salmon slices in a flat baking dish. Pour in the cool court bouillon to three-quarters of the depth of the salmon. Slowly bring the liquid to the boil (if using a glass or ceramic baking dish, place a heat-deflector pad under it). Cover and bake in oven for 10 minutes, or until the salmon flakes easily when pierced with a toothpick.

4. While cooking the salmon, reheat the sauce slowly. Lift the salmon onto a serving platter and remove the skin. Spoon some of the sauce over each slice and pass the rest separately.

SCALLOPS IN VEGETABLE BROTH

Some people may consider this a soup course. I serve it as a main course, since there are ample scallops to make it qualify for that role, and plan the rest of the meal accordingly: perhaps eggs baked in tomato shells as an opener, a cheese course to follow the scallops, and a dessert of baked fruit, pastry, or even mousse.

Serves 6

4 carrots
1 small to medium onion
2 leeks
1 celery rib
12 cups water
4 or 5 parsley sprigs, tied in a bundle
1 teaspoon thyme
½ teaspoon ground sage
½ teaspoon dried basil
dash of cayenne
1 teaspoon salt
1 teaspoon pepper
1 cup dry vermouth
2 pounds scallops, sliced in half crosswise if large

1. Cut the carrots, onion, leeks (white part only), and celery into julienne strips. Boil the water and add the vegetables along with the parsley, thyme, sage, basil, cayenne, salt, and pepper.

2. Simmer for 15 minutes. Add the vermouth and simmer for 10 minutes more. (The broth can be prepared in advance to this point and refrigerated.)

3. Remove the parsley bundle and bring the broth back to a rolling simmer. Add the scallops and cook 2 to 3 minutes. Ladle into individual soup bowls and serve at once.

SCALLOP BROCHETTES

Seafood and meat combinations are usually given the ungainly label of "surf 'n' turf." I find even the sound of it unappetizing, let alone what is generally put before you. But a subtle and sophisticated matching of land and sea foods is possible, as these brochettes prove.

Serves 6

3 pounds sea scallops (about 6 scallops per person)
3 shallots, finely chopped
salt and pepper
⅓ cup oil
¾ cup white wine
¼ cup brandy
5 or 6 parsley sprigs
3 ¼-inch-thick slices boiled ham
12 mushroom caps
6 tablespoons butter, melted
3 lemons, cut in half

1. Place the scallops in a flat dish and sprinkle with the shallots, salt, and pepper. Pour the oil, wine, and brandy over the scallops; they should be barely covered by the marinade, not swimming. Turn the scallops with your hands to coat all surfaces. Tuck in the parsley sprigs, cover, and put aside at room temperature for at least 1 hour, preferably 2. Mix scallops occasionally. Preheat the broiler.

2. Cut each ham slice into 12 squares. Dry the scallops on a towel. Thread 6 10-inch skewers, beginning with a mushroom cap (rounded side out), then alternating the scallops and ham squares, and finishing with another mushroom (again, rounded side out).

3. Place the skewers on the broiler grill pan, brush with butter, and broil 2 inches from the flame for about 2 minutes. Brush again with the butter and broil for another 2 minutes.

Turn the scallops and repeat the brushing and broiling. The final broiling time will be between 6 and 8 minutes depending on the size of the scallops; under no circumstances allow the scallops to overcook or they will become rubbery. Serve the brochettes on heated plates with lemon halves.

SAUTÉED SCALLOPS

Normally one doesn't think of marinating scallops because they are such good eating as is. But immersing them in just a bit of wine and oil plumps them into nuggets of incomparable sea flavor. There is another advantage to marinating: scallops of inferior quality and freshness are greatly improved.

Serves 6

2 pounds scallops
salt and pepper
½ cup oil (approximately)
1½ cups white wine (approximately)
butter and oil for frying
¼ cup chopped parsley
lemon wedges

1. Place the scallops in a large gratin dish or a similar one that will hold them in a single layer. Sprinkle with salt and pepper. Using ⅓ as much oil as wine, pour just enough oil and wine over scallops to cover them three-quarters of the way. Turn them with your hands to coat all surfaces with the marinade. Cover and refrigerate for at least 3 hours. (They will keep as long as 1 or 2 days.)
2. Using a large frying pan that will hold the scallops in a single layer or else 2 pans, melt enough butter with a little oil for ¼ inch of fat. When the fat is hot and foamy, lift the scallops out of the marinade, shake them sharply to drive off excess moisture, and add to the pan. Do not overcrowd the

pan or the scallops will not brown. Fry them for about 1 minute on each side, then transfer to a warm serving dish.

3. Pour off the cooking fat, add the marinade to the frying pan, and boil briskly for about half a minute. Season with salt and pepper and add the parsley. Spoon this sauce over the scallops and pass them with lemon wedges.

CRAB CAKES

Fresh crab meat is one of the great tastes of America. Its sweet, ocean-scented flavor makes every forkful cause for celebration. Precisely because of its own delicious goodness, cooks should do as little as possible to it. Many crab cake recipes call for all sorts of fillers to stretch the quantity. Don't. Indulge in them less often, but make them this way.

Serves 4

> 1 pound fresh backfin crab meat
> ½ cup mayonnaise, preferably homemade
> 1 tablespoon French mustard
> 1 egg
> juice of 1 lemon
> ½ teaspoon salt
> ¼ teaspoon pepper
> 2 tablespoons chopped parsley
> bread crumbs (optional)
> butter and oil for frying
> lemon wedges
> tartar sauce

1. Carefully pick over the crab meat without shredding it, keeping the meat in as large chunks as possible, and put the crab in a mixing bowl. In a small bowl beat together the mayonnaise, mustard, egg, lemon juice, salt, and pepper. Pour this sauce over the crab and, using your hands, gently mix it all

together. Sprinkle in the parsley, mix again, then chill for at least 1 hour.

2. Form the mixture into patties about ½ inch thick. If you like a browner crust, use the bread crumbs to coat the cakes. Spread some in a dish or on wax paper and carefully place each patty on the crumbs, then turn and pat the crumbs into the patty. Put the plain or crumbed cakes on wax paper or a dish and chill for another 15 minutes. There should be about 8 crab cakes.

3. In a large frying pan, melt a combination of enough butter and oil to stand no more than ¼ inch deep; these crab cakes are not to be deep-fried. When the fat is hot, fry the cakes a few at a time so as not to crowd the pan. Brown evenly on both sides, adding more fat as needed. The cakes are delicate, so turn them carefully. Serve warm with lemon wedges and tartar sauce. They are also delicious cold.

TURKEY BREAST WITH OYSTER SAUCE

The rationale for stuffing a turkey with oysters has always escaped me. During the long roasting the juices and fats of the turkey mask the flavor of the succulent bivalves. I decided to do a switch and put a briny sauce, complete with oysters, over thick slices of poached turkey breast. After preparing the sauce several ways, I found something decidedly right about the color and flavor of beef stock instead of chicken.

Serves 8

1 5-pound turkey breast or 2-pound boneless turkey breast
chicken stock or broth
1 onion, quartered
1 bay leaf, broken in half
1 celery rib, broken in half
salt and pepper

Sauce:
 4 tablespoons butter
 1 small onion, finely chopped
 1 celery rib with leaves, thinly sliced
 1/4 garlic clove, minced
 1/4 cup flour
 1/2 cup beef stock or broth
 1/2 cup clam juice
 pepper
 dash of Tabasco
 few drops gravy color (optional)

1 pint oysters (preferably small) with their liquor

1. Place the turkey breast in a deep casserole or pot. Pour in enough cold chicken stock or broth to completely cover the meat, then add the onion, bay leaf, celery, salt, and pepper. Slowly bring the stock to a simmer over medium heat. Partially cover the pot and gently cook the turkey breast for 45 minutes to 1 hour or until the juices run clear when meat is pierced with a small sharp knife.

2. Meanwhile, make the sauce. Melt the butter in a saucepan and add the onion, celery, and garlic; cover and simmer over medium heat for 10 minutes. Stir in the flour and cook for about 1 minute. While whisking, slowly pour in the beef stock and clam juice. The sauce will be very thick at this stage. Season with pepper and a good dash of Tabasco, plus a few drops of the gravy color, if desired. Cover and cook for 5 minutes. Add the oysters and their liquor and stir with a wooden spatula for just a minute or two until the oysters are lightly poached.

3. Drain the turkey breast well, cut into thick slices, and place them on dinner plates. Spoon sauce with oysters over each portion. Serve at once.

NOTE: The sauce can be prepared in advance without the oysters. Reheat the sauce at serving time and complete the recipe.

DUCK WITH GRAPEFRUIT

They may seem like a strange pair, but grapefruit and duck are a perfect match. Besides having a novel flavoring for duck, grapefruit's sharp acidity cuts through the richness of the meat.

Serves 4

> 4- to 5-pound duck
> salt and pepper
> 1 large grapefruit
> 2 tablespoons sugar
> 1/4 cup red wine vinegar
> 2 cups strong chicken broth
> 2 tablespoons arrowroot or cornstarch
> 1/4 cup Madeira or port
> 1/4 teaspoon aromatic bitters
> 2 teaspoons brandy

Preheat oven to 425 degrees.

1. With a vegetable peeler, remove the grapefruit rind, taking care not to include any of the bitter white pith. Cut the rind into long, thin slivers and put about a quarter of them inside the duck. Salt and pepper the cavity of the duck and truss it.

2. Put the duck, breast side up, on a rack in a roasting pan and prick the skin around the thighs, back, and lower breast. Roast for 5 minutes, then reduce the heat to 350 degrees and roast for about 1 1/4 hours, periodically turning the duck on its sides but finishing breast side up. To test for doneness, prick the thickest part of the thigh; if the juices that run out are pale pink the duck is medium rare. For well-done duck, roast until the juice runs pale yellow.

3. Meanwhile, boil the remaining slivered grapefruit rind in

water to cover for 15 minutes, drain at once, and run cold water over it. Let the rinds drain in a sieve and set aside.

4. Remove all the white pith of the grapefruit by cutting it away in long vertical slices. Cut the fruit sections from between the membranes and reserve the fruit.

5. In a small pot boil the sugar and vinegar until almost a caramel. Remove the pot from the heat and add the chicken broth slowly. Return the sauce to medium heat and simmer to melt the caramel, stirring with a wooden spatula.

6. In a small cup make a thin paste by mixing the arrowroot and Madeira. Add this paste to the sauce, whisking vigorously; then add the blanched grapefruit rind, bitters, and a little salt and pepper and simmer for 2 minutes. Drain the cooking juices from the roasted duck; strain them and remove all the fat. Add the degreased juices and brandy to the sauce and simmer for 1 minute more. Taste for seasonings and correct if necessary.

7. Slice the duck and place the pieces on a heated platter. Add the grapefruit sections to the sauce and bring to a boil. Spoon some of the sauce over the duck and pass the rest in a sauceboat.

TURKISH LAMB WITH LETTUCE

Spring lamb, with its slightly sweet flavor, is particularly appropriate for this cooking method. A deep casserole is necessary to accommodate what seems like an enormous amount of lettuce. Once heat hits it, though, it collapses to almost nothing.

Serves 8

3 bunches scallions (about 32), including green tops
1 onion, cut into 8 pieces
1 carrot, cut into 1-inch pieces
2 garlic cloves, sliced
2 large heads Boston lettuce
1 large head Romaine lettuce
salt and pepper
6 pounds lamb, cut into 2- to 3-inch pieces, with bone
2 tablespoons butter, cut into small pieces
1 tablespoon grated lemon rind
juice of 1 lemon
1 cup water

1. Cut the scallions into 3-inch lengths and scatter in the bottom of a deep casserole along with the onion, carrot, and garlic. Separate the lettuce leaves and layer them over the vegetables, sprinkling once or twice with a little salt and pepper.
2. Place the lamb pieces on top of the lettuce, lightly sprinkle with salt and pepper, and scatter the butter pieces over the meat.
3. Mix together the grated lemon rind, lemon juice, and water and pour over the lamb. Put a piece of aluminum foil directly over the lamb, then cover the pot closely and cook over low heat for about 2½ hours or until the meat is tender.

PAPILLOTE PORK CHOPS

One-dish cooking is an efficient way around kitchen cleanup chores. Papillote Pork Chops goes one step further and doesn't even dirty the dish! The whole main course—meat and vegetable accompaniments—is baked in individual foil packages, keeping all the good juices inside. If any liquid oozes onto the dish, it means the package wasn't sealed properly.

Serves 6

6 extra-thick pork chops
salt and pepper
3 medium onions
3 medium potatoes
3 medium tomatoes
3 bay leaves, broken in half
1½ teaspoons basil
6 tablespoons dry vermouth

Preheat oven to 375 degrees.

1. Trim extra fat from the chops. The chops can be browned before preparing the foil packages, but I prefer not to. Sprinkle the chops with salt and pepper and place each one on a large square of aluminum foil. Cut the onions, potatoes, and tomatoes into ½-inch-thick slices, trimming off the ends of the potatoes and onions to achieve even slices of all the vegetables.

2. On top of each pork chop lay a slice each of onion, potato, tomato, and a bay leaf half. Secure the vegetables to the meat by piercing through them with a toothpick (do not puncture the foil). Sprinkle each arrangement with salt and pepper and ¼ teaspoon basil. Extra slices of vegetables can be strewn around the chops.

3. Lift the edges of the foil upward and sprinkle 1 table-

spoon of vermouth over each package. Carefully fold over and crimp the edges of the foil to completely seal each package. Be careful not to pull the foil too tight and risk puncturing it with the meat bones or toothpicks.

4. Place the packages on a baking dish and bake for 1 hour. Transfer the meat and its vegetable garnish to a serving dish and spoon a little of the cooking juices over them.

SUNNY BRAISED PORK CHOPS

One could save washing one small pot by simply stirring the corn into the braising vegetables. The final taste will be about the same, but the presentation will suffer—the browned chops displayed on a bed of bright yellow corn look extremely appetizing.

Serves 6

> 6 thick pork chops (about ¾ inch thick)
> 5 to 8 tablespoons butter
> salt and pepper
> 2 green peppers
> 3 onions, thinly sliced
> 6 tablespoons whiskey (straight or blended)
> 2 tablespoons water
> 1 tablespoon mustard
> 2 cups vacuum-packed yellow corn kernels

1. Dry the pork chops on paper towels. In a large heavy skillet with a tight-fitting lid, melt 4 tablespoons of the butter. When the butter is hot and foamy, add the pork chops and brown both sides over medium-high heat. Sprinkle the chops with salt and pepper and remove to a dish.

2. If the butter has burned, pour it out and add an additional 3 tablespoons. Cut the green pepper flesh into pieces about ½ inch wide and 1 inch long. Add the peppers and the onions to

the skillet, stir well to coat with the melted butter, reduce the heat to medium, cover, and sauté the vegetables for 15 minutes.

3. Stir 3 tablespoons of whiskey and a little salt and pepper into the vegetables. Return the pork chops to the skillet, turn them quickly once or twice, reduce the heat to low, cover, and braise the chops for 15 minutes. Sprinkle in the remaining 3 tablespoons of whiskey, turn the chops, and simmer an additional 15 minutes.

4. In the meantime, heat the corn in a small pan, adding 1 tablespoon of butter, 1 tablespoon of water, and a little salt and pepper.

5. Mix the mustard with 1 tablespoon of water, add to the skillet, and stir well. Turn the chops several times to coat them with the light sauce.

6. Make a layer of the corn kernels on a warm serving platter. Arrange the pork chops on top and spoon the braising juices and vegetables over the chops.

STIR-FRIED PORK AND CAULIFLOWER

The many advantages of stir-frying have made this Chinese kitchen technique popular throughout the country. It is done very quickly, using very little fat. Which means that you put together a low-calorie and inexpensive dish in a flash. A wok is the best vessel for the cooking, but any deep heavy skillet can be used, preferably one with sloped sides. Rice, either boiled or fried, is the usual accompaniment.

Serves 6

½ pound lean pork, boneless
1 tablespoon cornstarch
⅓ cup soy sauce
½ cup dry sherry
1 teaspoon sugar
¾ cup chicken broth
½ head cauliflower
6 tablespoons oil
½ teaspoon salt

1. Tightly wrap the pork in plastic film and put it in the freezer for 30 minutes, then cut into very thin slices. (This light freezing firms the flesh and makes it possible to cut thinner slices.) In a bowl mix cornstarch with ¼ cup of soy sauce, ⅓ cup of sherry, the sugar, and ¼ cup chicken broth. Add the meat, mix with your hands to coat all slices, then put aside for 15 minutes. Drain the marinade and reserve it.

2. Meanwhile, pull apart the cauliflower florets and slice them as thin as possible. There should be about 4 cups of cauliflower slices.

3. Heat 3 tablespoons of oil in a heavy skillet or wok and, when it's quite hot, fry the drained pork slices over high heat, turning constantly. After a minute, pour in the marinade plus 1 tablespoon of soy sauce, 3 tablespoons of sherry, and another

¼ cup chicken broth. Cover and cook for 1 minute. Transfer to a bowl.

4. In the same skillet or wok, heat another 3 tablespoons of oil and, when it is very hot, add the cauliflower slices. Stir, turn, and toss the vegetable for about 3 minutes, then add the salt and the remaining ¼ cup of chicken broth. Turn heat down to medium, cover, and cook for another 2 or 3 minutes or just until the cauliflower is crisp-tender.

5. Return the meat and its sauce to the skillet, stir, cover, and cook for 1 minute more, just enough to reheat the meat.

CÔTES DE PORC À LA SAVOYARDE
(PORK CHOPS WITH ONIONS AND CHEESE)

Many easy-to-do dishes look as though they were thrown together, but no excuses are necessary for these pork chops. They arrive at the table beautifully crowned with a golden-brown dome of onions, cheese, and bread crumbs. No preliminary browning of the chops is necessary, which saves time during preparation and cleanup. Why Savoyarde? Because of the onions and cheese used in so many recipes in the *Haute-Savoie,* a picturesque, mountainous region in eastern France. Veal chops can be used in place of the pork; the procedure is the same.

Serves 6

7 tablespoons butter
1 medium onion, chopped
6 extra-thick (about 1½ inches thick) pork chops
salt and pepper
4 ounces grated Swiss cheese (about 1¼ cups)
½ cup bread crumbs
½ teaspoon sage
1 cup white wine
watercress for garnish

Preheat oven to 375 degrees.

1. Melt 2 tablespoons of butter in a small skillet, add the onions, cover, and cook over slow heat until they are soft, about 5 minutes. Meanwhile, trim excess fat from around the pork chops and sprinkle them liberally with salt and pepper, pressing the seasonings into the meat. Mix together in a bowl the cheese, bread crumbs, sage, salt, and pepper.

2. Divide the sautéed onions over the 6 chops, patting with the back of a spoon to make them more compact. Cover the onions with a thick coating of the cheese-and-bread-crumbs mixture, taking care to cover the entire surface of the chop. Press the topping a little with your hands to make it firmer.

3. Melt 3 tablespoons of butter. Meanwhile, use the remaining 2 tablespoons of butter to generously grease a baking dish that will hold the chops in a single layer. Place the chops in the dish, then slowly pour some melted butter over each chop. It is important to pour the butter slowly so that it is absorbed by the crumbs and does not roll off. Carefully pour about half the wine over the chops and the remainder into the bottom of the baking dish. Bake for about 35 minutes or until the topping is nicely browned; further baking will only make the chops dry. Transfer to a serving platter or to individual plates, spoon a little of the cooking juices over the chops, and garnish with the watercress.

HOT PORK ROLL

One showy facet of French cuisine is the *galantine*. This specialty requires boning a chicken, duck, turkey, or even a suckling pig, then stuffing the flat sack of meat and skin, and finally roasting or poaching it. Very impressive and very good it is, too. This Hot Pork Roll tips its hat to the Gallic original but eschews the tedious boning. Instead, lots of good flavors are rolled together in a cloth and poached in a good strong stock. Leftovers are delicious served cold.

2 pounds boned pork shoulder
½ pound lean ham
4 tablespoons butter
1 onion, finely chopped
2 garlic cloves, minced
2 slices white bread, with crusts
½ teaspoon thyme
¼ teaspoon nutmeg
½ teaspoon allspice
¼ teaspoon sage
½ teaspoon oregano
1 tablespoon salt
1 teaspoon pepper
2 eggs
½ cup sour cream
Mustard Sauce (pages 245–46)

For the poaching stock:
    bones from the pork
    3 cups chicken or turkey bones (approximately)
    chicken or turkey gizzards
    1 bay leaf
    1 carrot, cut into chunks
    1 tablespoon salt
    1 teaspoon pepper

1. Using either a grinder or food processor, grind together the pork, ham, and butter to a rather smooth consistency. Scrape the meats into a mixing bowl and add the onion and garlic. Grind the bread and add to the meats along with the thyme, nutmeg, allspice, sage, oregano, salt, and pepper. Mix very well with your hands. Beat together the eggs and sour cream, add to the meats, and mix again. Fry a teaspoon of the meat and taste. Correct the seasonings, if necessary. Chill.

2. While the meat is chilling, prepare the poaching stock. In a fish poacher or other long pot, put the pork bones, chicken or turkey bones and gizzards, the bay leaf, carrot, salt, and pepper. Add enough water to fill the pot two-thirds full. Bring

the water to a simmer and cook slowly, partially covered, for 20 minutes.

3. Select a strong dish towel with no holes or use 3 layers of cheesecloth. Stretch the cloth very flat. Scoop the chilled meat onto the towel along one end of the long edges and pat the meat into a long roll about 12 inches long and 3 inches in diameter. Roll the cloth tightly around the meat and tie the ends tightly with string. Poach the pork roll for about 45 minutes.

4. Lift the cooked roll from the stock and allow it to drip for 5 minutes. Cut off the string and carefully unroll the meat. Cut the roll into slices and place them in an overlapping row on a warm serving platter. Spoon some of the Mustard Sauce over the slices and pass the rest of the sauce separately.

NOTE: To prepare the Hot Pork Roll in advance, poach it as directed in the recipe, drain well, cool, and refrigerate, still wrapped. Refrigerate the poaching broth separately. At serving time bring the broth back to just below the simmering point, lower the pork roll into it, and reheat very gently for 15 to 20 minutes.

MIROTON DE BOEUF (GRATIN OF BEEF IN ONION SAUCE)

Thrifty French housewives have long known how to turn leftovers into delicious and completely new dishes. Here is one that begins with either boiled or roast beef and transforms it with a brisk, oniony topping.

Serves 6

6 tablespoons butter
3 medium onions, finely sliced
3 garlic cloves, minced
6 tablespoons flour

1½ cups beef broth
3 tablespoons vinegar
3 tablespoons tomato paste
salt and pepper
18 thin slices of cooked beef (about 1¼ pounds)
¾ cup bread crumbs
6 tablespoons grated Parmesan cheese

Preheat oven to 350 degrees.

1. Melt the butter in a skillet, add the onions and garlic, cover, and simmer gently for 7 to 10 minutes. Do not allow the onions to brown; stir from time to time.

2. Sprinkle in the flour and blend thoroughly. Add the beef broth, vinegar, tomato paste, salt, and pepper and simmer for about 20 minutes. If the sauce seems too thick add additional beef broth or water.

3. Pour half the sauce into a shallow baking dish and cover with the beef slices, then pour on the rest of the sauce. Sprinkle with the bread crumbs and cheese and bake for about 30 minutes or until the crumbs brown.

STIR-FRIED ASPARAGUS

At traditional Chinese banquets, each course is presented separately so that each dish can be appreciated without blurring the palate with another flavor. For the busy host or hostess who prepares and serves the meal without help, this may prove impractical. But there are certain dishes that should be spotlighted by themselves; stir-fried asparagus is one of them. These crunchy, bright green morsels can kick off a meal with a crisp note or refresh the taste buds after the meat dish. They also complement a cheese soufflé beautifully.

Serves 6

4 tablespoons vegetable oil
3 slices fresh ginger
10 peppercorns
2 unpeeled garlic cloves, mashed
1½ pounds fresh asparagus
1½ tablespoons soy sauce
2 tablespoons dark sesame seed oil (available in
   health-food stores and Oriental groceries)
2 tablespoons sherry
1 teaspoon sugar
½ teaspoon salt

1. Pour the vegetable oil into a wok or a heavy skillet with sloped sides. Add the ginger, peppercorns, and garlic, cover the pan, and heat slowly over low heat to brown the garlic and ginger. (This can be done well in advance.)
2. Snap off and discard the tough bottom sections of the asparagus. Rinse the stalks under cold water and with a sharp knife cut the stalks and points into long, thin diagonal slices, the longer the better.
3. In a small cup, stir together the soy sauce, sesame seed oil, sherry, sugar, and salt. Make sure that the sugar has dissolved.

4. With a skimmer, remove the flavorings from the oil and heat the oil to very hot. Add the asparagus and turn the pieces quickly with the skimmer and a large spoon to coat all the slices with the oil. Cover the wok for 30 seconds.

5. Pour in the seasoned soy sauce and mix again thoroughly to distribute the sauce. Cover again for 30 seconds or so. Test with a small, sharp knife by piercing the center of an asparagus slice. It should remain crunchy. Spoon into a deep serving dish and serve at once.

BAKED BEAN SPROUTS

Bean sprouts are usually stir-fried or mixed raw into salads. I find that baking them produces a mellow vegetable that makes a good partner for fried chops, roast chicken, and even omelets.

Serves 6

1½ pounds fresh bean sprouts
⅓ cup soy sauce
1 cup water
salt and pepper

Preheat oven to 350 degrees.

1. Rinse the sprouts and place them in a baking dish. In a small bowl, stir together the soy sauce, water, salt, and pepper. Pour over the sprouts.

2. Cover the dish and bake for about 30 minutes or until the sprouts are barely soft. Stir once or twice during the baking.

CABBAGE IN MILK

Even cabbage haters enjoy this mild and sweet transformation of the vegetable. The long cooking time thoroughly breaks down the fibers in the leaves and allows them to absorb most of the milk. Cabbage in Milk could be paired with steamed potatoes for a hearty vegetarian meal.

Serves 6 to 8

2-pound head of firm cabbage
1 quart milk (approximately)
salt and pepper
2 garlic cloves

1. Bring a large quantity of water to a boil. Meanwhile, cut the cabbage into quarters and remove the cores. Lightly salt the boiling water, add the cabbage, and cook for 5 minutes. Pour off the water and put the pot under cold running water to cool the cabbage. Squeeze as much water as possible out of each cabbage piece.
2. Place the cabbage in a deep, heavy nonreactive pot or a soufflé dish. Pour in enough milk to cover the cabbage and sprinkle with salt and pepper. Pierce the garlic cloves on toothpicks and add them to the milk. If using a pot, over medium heat bring the milk to a simmer, then reduce the heat to low. If using a soufflé dish, place it in a 375-degree oven. Simmer or bake for about 1½ hours, basting occasionally, until the cabbage is very soft and a brown crust covers the surface. Cut the quarters in half crosswise and spoon the leftover milk over each portion.

GINGERED CARROTS

Though fresh ginger enlivens the sauce for these carrots, it is used in a discrete fashion. Too often, strong flavorings overwhelm and upstage the vegetable; I believe that food should basically taste of itself.

Serves 6

1½ pounds baby carrots, or regular carrots cut into 2-inch
    chunks
6 slices fresh ginger
3 strips orange rind
¼ teaspoon sugar
salt and pepper
3 cups chicken broth (approximately)
3 tablespoons cornstarch

1. Place the carrots in a wide skillet that will hold them compactly in a single layer. With the flat side of a chef's knife, firmly press down on each ginger slice to bruise it and release its oils. Tuck the ginger and the orange rind among the carrots, then sprinkle with sugar, salt, and pepper. Pour in enough chicken broth to almost completely cover the carrots. Bring the broth to a boil, reduce the heat, cover, and simmer for 15 to 20 minutes, depending on the age of the carrots. They should be tender but with a hint of crispness left. (The carrots can be cooked ahead to this point and held until serving time.)

2. Remove the ginger and orange rind pieces. Stir about ⅔ cup of cold chicken broth into the cornstarch to make a paste. Pour it into the bubbling carrot liquid, stir, and cook for about 2 minutes or until the sauce turns from opaque to clear.

CAULIFLOWER WITH CAPER-BUTTER SAUCE

Traditionally this sauce is called *beurre noir* (black butter). In reality, it must not blacken, but cook just to a dark rich brown. It is also excellent with sautéed brains, poached fish or sweetbreads, sliced tongue, and such vegetables as brussels sprouts, small boiled potatoes, and string beans.

Serves 4 to 5

1 head cauliflower
4 tablespoons butter
2 tablespoons wine vinegar
2 tablespoons capers, rinsed and drained
1 tablespoon chopped parsley

1. Whole cauliflower makes the prettiest presentation, but it can also be cooked in florets. Boil the cauliflower in lightly salted water until just tender, drain well, and place in a deep dish.
2. Melt the butter in a small heavy saucepan until it turns dark brown. Immediately add the vinegar, capers, and parsley and bring to a boil. Spoon over the cauliflower.

BRAISED CELERY

Celery should come out of the salad bowl more often! Since it is in year-round supply, you can count on having it anytime you decide to prepare this particularly tasty version. It goes with most roast meats or fowl and is particularly good with pork.

Serves 6

3 bunches celery
1½ cups dry white wine
1 cup chicken broth
2 tablespoons chopped fresh basil or 1 tablespoon dried
  basil
salt and pepper
6 tablespoons butter
2 tablespoons chopped parsley

1. Cut off most of the root end of the celery, leaving just enough to hold the vegetable together. Cut off the leafy tops and reserve for another use. The trimmed celery should measure 4 to 5 inches long. Rinse the celery under cold water and place in a large, flat-bottomed nonreactive pan that will hold all the celery snugly.

2. Pour in the wine and chicken broth, then sprinkle the basil, salt, and pepper over the top. Bring the liquid to a fast simmer, cover, and braise for 15 to 20 minutes or until the celery is crisply tender. Test for doneness with a small, sharp knife. Drain the celery at once, plunge it into cold water, and drain again.

3. Squeeze the celery to remove excess water and cut stalks in half lengthwise. Melt the butter in the skillet, add the celery, and turn it several times to coat with the butter. Cover and simmer gently for 5 minutes, then sprinkle with parsley and cook 1 minute longer.

4. Remove the braised celery to a serving dish, spooning extra butter over the vegetable.

NOTE: The braising liquid can be reserved for poaching other vegetables or used as a stock for soups.

CELERI-RAVE NIÇOISE (CELERY ROOT WITH OLIVES)

One almost never sees celery root in any form other than julienned and tossed with a mustardy mayonnaise, though it also has wonderful cooking possibilities. The root's tingly freshness marries well with many flavors, as this recipe illustrates. Oil-cured olives are the best, but even California's mild variety adds snap to the dish.

Serves 5 or 6

1¾- to 2-pound celery root
2 tablespoons olive oil
1 cup pitted black olives
1 tablespoon butter
1 tablespoon flour
¼ cup tomato paste
1 to 1¼ cups chicken broth
½ teaspoon basil
salt and pepper

1. Using a stainless steel knife, trim the celery root by first removing a slice each from the top and bottom, then stand it upright. Make vertical cuts around the root to remove the fibrous skin. Turn the root over and trim away the remaining skin. (There is a good deal of waste in the trimming—as much as 4 to 7 ounces can be lost.) Cut the root in half, cut slices about ½ inch thick, and cut these slices into pieces about ½ inch square.

2. Heat the olive oil in a nonreactive skillet, add the celery root pieces, and turn them with a wooden spoon to coat all surfaces with oil. Cover and cook over medium heat for 15 minutes or until tender. While the celery root is sautéing, boil the olives in water for 5 minutes, drain well, and rinse with cold water. When celery root is tender, with a slotted spoon remove it to a bowl. Wipe out the skillet.

3. Melt the butter in the skillet and, when it's hot and foamy, stir in the flour. Cook for 1 minute, then add the tomato paste and stir for another minute. Add 1 cup chicken broth, basil, and a little salt and pepper. Cover the skillet and simmer the sauce slowly for 5 minutes. Add the celery root and olives, mix well, cover, and cook for another five minutes. If you would like a thinner sauce, add the remaining ¼ cup chicken broth.

CELERY ROOT PUREE

Celery root is most readily available in fall and winter, just when game comes to the table. Together they make memorable eating.

Serves 6

3 pounds celery root
2 eggs
¼ cup sour cream
¼ cup milk
salt and pepper
nutmeg
2 tablespoons butter, cut into pieces

1. Trim the celery root according to the directions for Celery Root Niçoise (pages 220–21). Cut it into slices or chunks and drop into a pot of cold water. Bring the water to a boil, add a little salt, and cook for about 20 minutes or until the pieces are soft. Drain very well.
2. Puree the celery root in a food processor or beat it to a puree with an electric beater. With the motor running, add the eggs one at a time, then the sour cream and milk.
3. Scrape the puree into a heavy saucepan and add the salt, pepper, a good grating of nutmeg, and the butter. Reheat over low heat, stirring, until the butter has melted.

BRAISED ONIONS

The olive oil used in the braising liquid gives the onions a silken texture as well as extra flavor. This is an excellent vegetable to serve with roast meats. To save oven heat and working time, braise some extra onions for another day. Simmer them for 5 minutes in a tomato sauce and you will have a completely different dish.

Serves 6

6 onions
¾ cup olive oil
3 to 4 cups water
2 teaspoons salt

Preheat oven to 375 degrees.
1. Peel onions, cut in half, and place in a shallow baking dish that will hold them snugly. Mix together the olive oil, 3 cups of water, and salt and pour over the onions. They should be almost covered; if not, add more water.
2. Cover the dish and bake for about 45 minutes or until soft.

ECHALOTES ROTIES (ROASTED SHALLOTS)

These roasted shallots will add an unexpected element to any meal. Generally this mild member of the onion family is regarded as a flavoring for sauces and braised dishes, but just as onions can be baked whole in their skins, so can shallots. No preparation whatsoever is necessary; they are simply tossed into a roasting pan about 20 minutes before the meat or chicken is finished. The shallots emerge intact, a little limp on the outside but soft and buttery inside.

Shallots, allow 3 or 4 per person

1. Add the shallots to a roasting pan containing meat or chicken. Turn once or twice during the roasting. They should be soft in about 20 minutes in a 350-degree oven.

2. The guests peel the shallots on the dinner plate by holding the root end with the fork and gently pressing the soft flesh out with a knife.

NOTE: To enjoy roasted shallots when not preparing roast meat or chicken, simply pour some melted butter, goose or chicken fat, or even lard over them. Turn the shallots to coat them with the fat and bake, uncovered, for 20 minutes in a 350-degree oven.

PARSLEY FRITTERS

These puffy little fritters are unusual in their spring-fresh flavor and light texture. Once fried they will stay souffléed until they are devoured.

Makes about 12 2-inch fritters

8 cups parsley leaves, lightly packed
4 egg yolks
¼ cup sour cream
2 tablespoons flour
pinch of nutmeg
salt and pepper
2 scallions, including green tops, finely chopped
2 tablespoons Parmesan cheese
2 egg whites
pinch of cream of tartar
oil for frying

1. Bring a large quantity of water to a boil, add the parsley leaves, and as soon as the water returns to a boil, stir the

leaves and immediately drain into a colander. Cool under cold running water. Squeeze the water out of the parsley a handful at a time, then fluff out the leaves by separating them with your fingers.

2. In a bowl, whisk together the egg yolks, sour cream, flour, a healthy pinch of nutmeg, salt, and pepper. Add the scallions, parsley, and Parmesan and stir all together with a wooden spatula. (The batter can wait at this stage for several hours before finishing the fritters; keep covered.)

3. Beat the egg whites until they are soft and foamy, then sprinkle in a pinch of cream of tartar and continue beating until stiff peaks are formed. Using the wooden spatula, thoroughly fold about a third of the beaten whites into the parsley batter. Lightly fold in the remaining whites with a rubber spatula; do not overmix.

4. Pour oil into a large skillet to a depth of no more than ¼ inch; you really want just a good film of oil in the pan. Heat the oil, then spoon in a heaping tablespoon of parsley batter for each fritter. Fry for about half a minute on each side and remove to a warm plate lined with paper towels. Keep the fritters warm while frying the rest of the batter.

PEAS WITH MUSHROOMS

The sweet taste of fresh spring peas is a pleasure that we can seldom enjoy. By the time the pods hit retail markets they usually have been around awhile and the pea's natural sugars have largely turned to starch. If you cannot obtain truly sweet fresh peas, you may substitute frozen ones. Here is one way to further brighten their flavor.

Serves 5 to 6

1 10-ounce package frozen peas
2 cups mushrooms (about ¼ pound), sliced
grated rind of 1 lemon

salt and pepper
½ cup chicken broth
2 tablespoons butter, cut into pieces

1. Put the peas and mushrooms in a small pot. Sprinkle on the grated lemon rind, salt, and pepper, and pour in the chicken broth.
2. Bring the broth to a boil, cover, reduce the heat, and simmer for 3 minutes. Lift the vegetables out of the pot with a slotted skimmer and transfer them to a warm serving dish. Add the butter and mix until it has melted. Serve hot.

OVEN-BRAISED POTATOES

This almost simpleminded recipe comes from a most unlikely source—the kitchen of a posh Parisian hotel. In this method, thick slices of potatoes are almost completely covered with water and baked in a very hot oven. As the water boils off, the interior of the potato becomes moist and extremely tender. It produces the best-tasting potatoes imaginable.

Serves 6

4 russet potatoes
3 tablespoons butter (approximately)
water
salt and pepper

Preheat oven to 450 degrees.
1. Peel the potatoes and cut off a slice from each end, then slice them horizontally into 1-inch-thick pieces. It is important that all slices be of the same thickness so that they will cook uniformly.
2. Place the slices snugly in a single layer either in a heavy skillet or a baking dish; do not use too large a dish. Spread about ½ teaspoon of butter over each slice. Pour in enough

water to come almost to the top of the slices and sprinkle with salt and pepper.

3. Bring the water to the simmering point (if using a baking dish, place it on a heat-deflector pad), then bake for about 45 minutes. By this time the water should have boiled off almost completely and the potato slices should be soft when pierced with a sharp knife. If not done, add a little more water and bake for 10 minutes more. The potato slices will be nicely browned.

GOLDEN POTATO GRATIN

Because of their mealy texture, russet potatoes are usually used for baking but little else. Though regular potatoes can be used for this gratin, the russet brings to it a most desirable texture.

Serves 6

1 to 1¼ cups milk
1½ pounds potatoes, preferably russet, peeled and
    coarsely grated
1 small onion, chopped
salt and pepper
oil
1 egg yolk
½ cup cream
2 tablespoons Parmesan cheese

Preheat oven to 400 degrees.

1. While bringing the milk to the boiling point, mix the potatoes and onion together in a mixing bowl and season with salt and pepper. Oil a 9-inch pie dish, scoop the potatoes into it, and smooth into an even layer. Pour in enough hot milk to almost cover the potatoes. Cover and bake for 15 minutes.

2. Beat together the egg yolk, cream, and Parmesan cheese and season well with pepper. Uncover the baking dish and spoon the egg yolk-cream topping over the surface. Return potatoes to the oven for 15 minutes or until the topping has puffed a little and is nicely browned. Serve at once.

OVEN *ROESTI*

Roesti, boiled potatoes grated and fried into a crunchy pancake, is as much a national dish in Switzerland as the better-known cheese fondue. Occasionally a little grated onion is added. I've changed the procedure to eliminate the constant attention a true *roesti* demands by baking this version in a very hot oven. Handle the skillet with great care.

Makes 1 10-inch pancake

> 1 pound potatoes, boiled in skins
> 5 tablespoons butter
> salt and pepper
> oil

Preheat oven to 475 degrees.

1. Skin the potatoes and coarsely grate them into a mixing bowl. Melt 4 tablespoons of the butter and pour over the potatoes. Sprinkle with salt and pepper and toss to thoroughly coat the potatoes with the butter and seasonings.

2. Oil a 10-inch cast-iron skillet and place it in the hot oven for a minute or two. Using heavy pot holders, remove the skillet from the oven, then scrape in the potatoes and pat them into an even layer. Cut the remaining tablespoon of butter into small pieces and scatter over the top. Place in the oven, uncovered.

3. There are two presentations possible. First, the *roesti* can be baked for 20 minutes, then reversed onto a serving dish so

that the brown crust is on top. Or, in a version truer to the original, after 15 minutes reverse the pancake onto a flat lid and slide it back into the skillet, then bake for an additional 10 minutes to produce a crust on the second side as well. Cut into wedges.

SAUERKRAUT AND PRUNES

Plain old sauerkraut takes on almost fancy airs when embellished with prunes and white wine. This makes an excellent accompaniment for all pork, ham, and sausage dishes. If you would like a sweet-and-sour note, add the optional sugar.

Serves 6

½ cup (about 3 ounces) pitted prunes, rinsed
1 cup white wine
2 tablespoons oil
1 onion, chopped
1 pound sauerkraut, rinsed and drained well
2 tablespoons sugar (optional)
2 beef bouillon cubes
pepper
2 garlic cloves

1. Put the prunes in a small heat-resistant bowl. Bring the wine just to the boiling point, pour over the prunes, cover, and put aside for at least 1 hour.
2. Heat the oil in a nonreactive skillet, add the onion, cover, and fry slowly until wilted, about 5 minutes. Do not allow the onions to brown. Add the sauerkraut and the sugar if desired, crumble in the bouillon cubes, and grind in lots of pepper. Cook for about 1 minute while stirring.
3. Add the prunes and their soaking wine. Pierce the garlic on toothpicks and tuck into the sauerkraut. Cover and simmer slowly for about 45 minutes. Remove the garlic and serve.

TRICOLOR VEGETABLE CASSEROLE

The natural juices of the baking vegetables provide all the moisture necessary for this casserole. Those same juices also unite the varying flavors of the vegetable medley into a dish of subtle yet distinctive character. Serve it with roasts or grilled meats or chicken.

Serves 5 to 6

3/4 pound potatoes (about 3), thinly sliced
salt and pepper
1 onion, thinly sliced
3/4 pound yellow squash (2 or 3), thinly sliced
3 tablespoons butter
2 tomatoes, cut into 1/4-inch slices

Preheat oven to 350 degrees.

1. Select a shallow baking dish that holds about 1 quart. Butter the dish liberally, then layer in half the potatoes and sprinkle them with salt and pepper. Make a layer of half the onions over the potatoes, and top the onions with half the squash slices. Sprinkle the squash with salt and pepper and dot with half the butter.

2. Repeat with another layer of potatoes, onions, and squash, seasoning as before. Finally, place the tomato slices on top and press down lightly on them. Sprinkle very lightly with salt. Cover the dish closely and bake for about 1 1/4 hours or until the potatoes are soft when pierced with a knife.

CREAMY TURNIPS

Please note that these turnips are not creamed, but creamy. Tangy yogurt is stirred into the sauce, underscoring the crisp flavor of the turnips. The yogurt provides a smooth consistency without a heavy richness.

Serves 6

1½ pounds turnips, preferably small ones
½ onion, thinly sliced
1½ cups chicken broth
salt and pepper
½ cup yogurt
2 tablespoons cornstarch

1. Peel the turnips and cut them into slices a shade thinner than ¼ inch. Place the turnips in a pot, add the onions, and toss the two vegetables together. Pour in the chicken broth, then sprinkle with salt and pepper. Bring the broth to a simmer, cover, and cook for about 10 minutes or until the turnips are just tender.

2. Measure the yogurt into a bowl, add the cornstarch, and stir them until the cornstarch is thoroughly blended into the yogurt. Stir the yogurt mixture into the chicken broth and cook slowly for about 5 minutes or until the sauce thickens.

NOTE: The turnips and onions can be cooked ahead. At serving time, reheat the vegetables and complete the recipe with the yogurt and cornstarch addition.

GRILLED HERBED TOMATOES

One of the easiest ways to garnish and flavor tomatoes at the same time is to take advantage of the soft spreadable herb cheeses available in most markets. Some are touched with garlic, others not, but all are full of dense herb aromas that make the cheese a perfect tomato topping. Even almost-useless winter tomatoes can be salvaged this way.

Serves 6

2/3 cup herb-flavored soft cheese
3 tablespoons cream
3 ripe tomatoes, room temperature

1. In a small bowl cream together the cheese and the cream until soft and smooth. Cut the tomatoes in half horizontally and spread each half with the creamed cheese. Place on a baking dish. (The garnished tomatoes can stand at room temperature for 1 hour, or in the refrigerator for up to 3 hours. In the latter case, they should be removed from the refrigerator 20 minutes before broiling.)
2. Place the baking dish under a preheated broiler for about 2 minutes or until the top is bubbly and browned in spots. Serve piping hot.

WILD RICE WITH MUSHROOMS

Although wild rice seems an extravagance these days, like real rice (wild rice is actually a grass) it expands threefold, which means that a little goes a long way. But the very best reason for serving wild rice is that nothing else tastes quite like it.

Serves 6

1 cup wild rice
3 cups chicken broth or water
salt
4 tablespoons butter
¼ pound mushrooms, sliced
pepper
nutmeg

1. Rinse the wild rice in a strainer and dump it into a deep pot. Cover with the chicken broth or water (or a combination), add 1 teaspoon of salt, and bring the liquid to a boil. Reduce the heat and simmer for about 25 minutes, or until the grains burst open and are tender. Stir occasionally during the cooking. Drain well.
2. While the rice is cooking, melt the butter in a skillet and add the sliced mushrooms. Sauté the mushrooms for 2 or 3 minutes and season with salt and pepper to taste.
3. Scrape the cooked wild rice into a mixing bowl and add the mushrooms and melted butter. Season with freshly grated nutmeg, salt, and pepper.

APRICOT-ORANGE CREAM

This final suave note to a dinner party is best served in small portions. The dried apricots and cream both give it richness. I prefer to serve it in small cups similar to the French *pots de crème*. Any small container will do, and if need be, even paper-lined foil cups can be used.

Serves 8 to 10

½ pound dried apricots
1 seedless orange
½ cup orange juice
⅓ to ½ cup sugar
1½ cups heavy cream

2 tablespoons orange liqueur
Garnish: Candied Orange Rind (pages 240–41) or candied
    violets (optional)

1. Rinse the apricots, put them in a saucepan, cover with boiling water, and let stand for 30 minutes, covered. With a swivel-bladed vegetable peeler, remove the rind from the orange, being careful not to take with it the bitter white pith. Cut the rind into pieces. Cut away all the white pith from the orange, then cut the fruit into chunks and drop into the bowl of a food processor or blender. Add the orange juice and rind and puree. Some of the rind will remain in small pieces, but don't worry about it.

2. Drain the apricots and pour the orange puree over them, then add enough water to just cover the apricots. Bring the liquid to a simmer, cover, and cook for 15 minutes. Add ¹⁄₃ cup sugar and cook, uncovered, another 15 minutes, stirring often, until most of the liquid has been absorbed or evaporated. Taste for sugar and add the additional 3 tablespoons if desired. Cool the mixture.

3. Scrape the cooked apricots into the food processor, add ¹⁄₂ cup cream and the orange liqueur, and puree. (If using a blender, process only half the puree and cream at a time.)

4. Using a chilled bowl and chilled beaters, whip the remaining 1 cup cream until quite firm. Thoroughly fold about a third of the whipped cream into the puree, then lightly fold in the rest.

5. Spoon the Apricot-Orange Cream into small cups, allowing about ¹⁄₂ cup per serving. Cover and chill for at least 3 hours. At serving time, garnish each portion with a candied violet or candied orange peel.

NOTE: Apricot-Orange Cream can easily be made the day before and chilled until serving.

LEMON MOUSSE

The sparkling fresh flavor of lemon is always welcome at the end of a meal. This pale-golden mousse capitalizes on that palate-awakening note by restraining the sugar and staying just this side of tart. The optional addition of gelatin insures a firm texture; if the weather is hot or your refrigerator is over-crowded it is wise to add it. Without it the mousse has a more delicate texture.

Serves 6

½ cup lemon juice
1 tablespoon gelatin (optional)
4 eggs, at room temperature
⅔ cup sugar
2 tablespoons butter, cut into pieces
1 egg white, at room temperature
pinch of cream of tartar

1. Put the lemon juice in a small pot. If not using gelatin, proceed to step 2. If using gelatin, sprinkle it in and put juice aside for 5 minutes. Then place the pot on low heat and stir until the mixture just reaches the simmering point and turns clear, indicating that the gelatin has dissolved. Put aside.

2. Separate the eggs and put the yolks in a large mixing bowl. With an electric beater, beat the yolks for a minute or so, then begin to slowly add the sugar, beating constantly. Beat until the mixture is light in color and creamy.

3. Add the butter to the yolks and suspend the bowl over simmering water in a pot. Heat the mixture slowly, beating constantly, until the butter melts. Add the lemon juice and beat for another 2 minutes.

4. If using the gelatin, you can use a 4-cup soufflé dish and build up its sides with an aluminum foil collar to create a more dramatic presentation. Otherwise, use a 6-cup soufflé dish. Combine the extra egg white with the 4 that were separated

and begin beating them. When the whites are soft and foamy, add a large pinch of cream of tartar, and beat until the whites are stiff. Using a whisk, fold about a third of the whites into the lemon base. Gently fold in the rest of the whites with a rubber spatula, then spoon into the soufflé dish. Refrigerate for at least 3 hours. At serving time, remove the foil collar, if used.

ORANGES CYRANO

This velvety dessert is traditionally presented in orange shells, although you can use one 4- to 5-cup mold. I've made a change from the standard recipe by using half the amount of cream and adding egg whites, since I discovered that egg white does not reduce the natural flavor of the orange as much as rich cream does. Of course, you may use a full cup of cream if you prefer.

Serves 6 to 7

6 large navel oranges
½ cup extra orange juice, if necessary (approximately)
1 to 1¼ cups sugar
1½ tablespoons gelatin
1 to 2 tablespoons orange liqueur
½ cup heavy cream
2 egg whites, at room temperature
Garnish: 6 crystallized violets, angelica or mint sprigs
  (optional)

1. About a quarter of the way down, cut a cap off each orange. Use a sturdy spoon to scrape all the orange pulp out of the shells and the caps. (It is important to get all the pulp out of the shells or it could dilute the filling later.) Squeeze the pulp, saving the juice; if there is less than two cups of juice, add enough extra orange juice to fill out. Add 1 cup of sugar and stir until it dissolves. Put aside for 15 minutes, then taste for sweetness and add additional sugar, if desired. Keep in mind that the cream and egg whites will soften the sweetness some-

what. Put the orange shells in one plastic bag and the caps in another and chill.

2. Pour about ½ cup of the orange juice into a small pot, sprinkle in the gelatin, and put aside for 5 minutes. Then gently heat over a low flame until the gelatin dissolves, stirring constantly. Cool slightly, then readd mixture to the rest of the orange juice. Chill the juice until it just begins to thicken.

3. Beat the heavy cream until stiff, then fold into the syrupy orange juice. Chill for 5 minutes. Beat the egg whites until stiff and delicately fold them into the orange juice mixture.

4. Spoon the mixture into the chilled orange shells, rounding the tops nicely. Chill for at least 3 hours.

5. At serving time, place a crystallized violet on each dessert and cover with a cap that has been decorated with a sprig of angelica or fresh mint.

MERINGUE "CAKE"

Meringue "Cake" isn't really a cake at all but a less-sweet meringue baked in a cake shape. It puffs as beautifully as a soufflé in the oven, but collapses a bit as it cools. No problem. The sauce that covers its surface camouflages any holes or cracks.

Serves 6

1 cup sugar
⅔ cup water
8 egg whites, at room temperature
½ teaspoon cream of tartar
1 tablespoon vanilla
¼ teaspoon almond extract
2 tablespoons corn syrup
3 tablespoons cornstarch
Caramel Sauce (pages 250–51)

Preheat oven to 325 degrees.

1. In a small pot, boil ¾ cup of sugar and the water together for 5 minutes. Meanwhile, in a large bowl begin beating the egg whites with an electric beater. When the whites are soft and foamy, add the cream of tartar and beat until the whites are firm.

2. Pour the boiling syrup over the egg whites while continuing to beat at a fast speed. Beat for 2 minutes or until the egg whites form stiff peaks. Add the vanilla, almond extract, and corn syrup and beat again for another half a minute.

3. Mix the cornstarch with the remaining ¼ cup of sugar to hold the starch in suspension, allowing for more even distribution. Sprinkle the sugar-cornstarch mixture over the surface of the beaten whites and fold in gently with a rubber spatula.

4. Butter an 8- to 10-cup soufflé dish, then fit a circle of wax paper on the bottom and butter it. Scoop the meringue into the dish and smooth the top with a spatula.

5. Put the soufflé dish in a water bath and bake for 45 minutes to 1 hour or until the meringue puffs and begins pulling away from the sides. Remove from the oven and cool.

6. Cut around the sides of the dish with a flexible knife. Dip the bottom of the dish in hot water for a few seconds, then use a flexible spatula to gently lift around the bottom edges. Place a serving platter over the soufflé dish and reverse, shaking sharply to dislodge the "cake." Pour several spoonfuls of Caramel Sauce over the top of the meringue and pass the rest at the table. Use two large spoons to cut portions of the Meringue "Cake."

NOTE: Meringue "Cake" can be made the day before serving. After it cools and shrinks a little, it will not shrink any more. Keep it in its dish in a cool dry spot, very loosely covered.

WINTER PEACH ICE CREAM

The best of all fruit desserts are made in the summertime when fruits are at peak flavor. But as the long winter months stretch on, one often desires some hint of summer's bounty. Here is one way to satisfy that yearning.

Makes about 1 quart

2 eggs
1 cup heavy cream
2 teaspoons orange liqueur
2 10-ounce packages frozen sweetened peaches, not
    defrosted

1. Put the eggs, cream, and liqueur in a blender or food processor and process for a few seconds. Add chunks of the frozen sliced peaches, blending well after each addition. There will be 4 cups of puree.
2. Pour the puree into a bowl and place it in the freezer. After about 2 hours when the mixture is mushy, beat well, then return to freeze completely, at least 3 hours. Remove from the freezer 10 minutes before serving.

FROZEN PUMPKIN PIE

This definitely is not a pumpkin pie for Thanksgiving dinner as it is far too rich to follow the traditional feast. But after any sensible meal, it is a triumph.

Makes 1 9-inch pie

1 to 1½ cups cooked pumpkin, fresh or canned
½ cup brown sugar
½ teaspoon salt

1 teaspoon cinnamon
¼ teaspoon ginger
⅛ teaspoon cloves
1 quart vanilla ice cream, softened
1 9-inch graham cracker pie shell (page 249)
Topping: whipped cream and pecans (optional)

1. Combine the pumpkin, sugar, salt, and spices and beat very well. Fold the pumpkin into the softened ice cream, then scoop into the pie shell and smooth the surface. Freeze for at least 3 hours.

2. Remove the pie from the freezer about ½ hour before serving. Garnish with the whipped cream and nuts if desired.

FROZEN GRAHAM CRACKER CREAM

Beyond being formed into pie shells, graham cracker crumbs are seldom used in the kitchen. Here is a new way to think about them. This frozen dessert certainly could be made in one large mold, but I find it a nicer touch to prepare individual servings.

Serves 6

6 tablespoons graham cracker crumbs
2 tablespoons sugar
pinch of salt
6 tablespoons milk
½ tablespoon corn syrup
½ cup heavy cream
⅛ teaspoon vanilla
⅛ to ¼ teaspoon orange- or chocolate-flavored liqueur

1. Chill beaters and bowl for whipping the cream. Pour the crumbs into a small bowl and add the sugar, salt, and milk. Let stand for 1 hour. The crumbs will absorb most of the milk and become mushy. Stir in the corn syrup.

2. Place 6 paper-lined foil cups on a small baking sheet or flat dish that is freezer-proof. Using the chilled bowl and beaters, beat the cream until very thick; add the vanilla and liqueur and beat another 10 seconds.

3. Scoop about a third of the whipped cream over the crumbs and fold in very thoroughly to lighten the mushy mixture. Then scrape the crumb mixture over the rest of the whipped cream and fold together thoroughly but lightly.

4. Use a small ladle or a pitcher to fill the cups two-thirds full with the cream. Freeze for at least 5 hours. Remove from the freezer about 10 minutes before serving.

CANDIED ORANGE PEEL

Candied Orange Peel adds a pretty, curly note on top of poached pears, crêpes, custards, bananas, and many other compatible sweets. The peel can be candied anytime you are using oranges and have no need for the skins. Once prepared they keep for weeks in the refrigerator in a tightly covered container.

> orange peel
> water
> sugar
> corn syrup

1. With a swivel-bladed vegetable peeler, carefully remove the rind from the oranges, making certain that none of the white pith is included. Cut the rind into very thin julienne and place in a small, heavy pot.

2. Cover the orange peels with 2 inches of water, bring to a boil, and simmer for 15 minutes. Drain the rinds thoroughly and return to the pot.

3. Pour in enough water to cover the peel by ½ inch, measuring the amount of water you add. For each ½ cup of water, add 3 tablespoons of sugar and 1 tablespoon of corn

syrup. Bring to a boil over moderately high heat, cover, and simmer for 10 minutes.

4. Remove the lid, reduce the heat to a simmer, and continue cooking until all the water has evaporated and the peel is coated with a light syrup. Stir occasionally at the beginning of the cooking and more often as the water level is reduced. Cool the candied peel. Spoon it into a small container, cover tightly, and refrigerate until needed.

Accompanying Recipes

Though there are only a dozen entries in this section, they are meant to be used over and over with other recipes. Mix and match the three pie crusts with any of the fillings in this or other books. Pour Caramel Sauce inside and over warm crêpes, then grill for a few moments. Spoon Raspberry Sauce over ice-cold sliced oranges, or warm it and use with crêpes. The savory sauces can be allied with any number of meats and vegetables. In short, don't always judge a chapter by its length.

TOMATO SAUCE

Makes 1¹/₂ cups

2 tablespoons olive oil
¹/₂ cup coarsely chopped onion
14-ounce to 1-pound can tomatoes, preferably Italian plum
¹/₄ teaspoon oregano
¹/₄ teaspoon basil
¹/₄ teaspoon fennel seeds
salt and pepper
1 tablespoon butter, at room temperature

1. In a covered saucepan simmer the oil and onion together for about 5 minutes. Add the tomatoes with their juice and all the spices; partially cover and simmer for 30 minutes.
2. Pour the sauce through a sieve and push the tomato pulp through with a pestle or the back of a wooden spoon. Discard the fibers and pulp remaining in the sieve. Add the butter to the still-hot sauce and stir until it melts.

NOTE: This Tomato Sauce will keep in the refrigerator for a week and in the freezer for six months. Add the butter when reheating the sauce.

PESTO (BASIL-GARLIC SAUCE)

In addition to pairing *Pesto* with Spaghetti Squash (page 155), keep this pungent mixture on hand for pasta as well. A small amount of it will also enliven any number of sauces and vegetable preparations. Make it in summer when basil is in full leaf. It freezes perfectly, but the cheese should not be added when making the *pesto;* instead, stir it in after defrosting.

Makes 1¹/₂ to 2 cups

2 cups fresh basil leaves
2 to 3 teaspoons chopped garlic
1 teaspoon salt
½ teaspoon black pepper
¼ cup pine nuts, walnuts, or cashews
1 to 1½ cups olive oil
½ cup freshly grated Parmesan or Romano cheese

1. Put the basil leaves, garlic, salt, and pepper in the bowl of a food processor and process in short bursts to chop the leaves and reduce their volume. Add the nuts and repeat the chopping for half a minute. With the motor running, slowly add the oil in a thin stream until the sauce is thin enough to drop easily from a spoon.

2. Add the cheese and process until smooth. Refrigerate or freeze in a tightly covered container, but bring back to room temperature before using.

MUSTARD SAUCE

This sauce has a good deal of snap to it already, but for cooks who are addicted to the fire of Szechwan cooking, a full tablespoon of the dry mustard is tolerable.

Makes ¾ cup

1 teaspoon salt
1 tablespoon sugar, or to taste
⅛ teaspoon pepper
2 teaspoons dry mustard
1 teaspoon cornstarch
1 egg
½ cup water
¼ cup vinegar

1. In a small pot combine the salt, sugar, pepper, dry mustard, and cornstarch. In a bowl beat the egg, water, and vinegar together, then stir into the dry ingredients and blend well.

2. Cook over medium heat, stirring often, until the sauce thickens, about 3 minutes. Serve hot or cold.

CRÊPES

Makes about 12 crêpes

¾ cup flour
1 egg, plus 1 yolk
pinch of salt
1 to 1¼ cups milk, at room temperature
1 tablespoon sugar (optional, for dessert-crêpes)
4 tablespoons butter (approximately)

1. Put the flour in a mixing bowl and make a well in the center. Place the egg, egg yolk, salt, and about ½ cup milk in the well. Using a wire whisk, blend together the eggs and milk, then slowly incorporate the flour. Beat the batter until it seems to pull and makes an occasional bubble. Beat in another ½ cup milk. Beat in the sugar if desired for dessert crêpes. Cover and put aside at room temperature for at least ½ hour, preferably 1 hour.

2. Melt 2 tablespoons of butter in a crêpe pan, then stir it into the batter; if the mixture seems too thick, add the remaining ¼ cup milk.

3. Melt a little butter in the pan; when hot pour in about 3 tablespoons of batter and swirl immediately to cover the bottom surface with a film. When it has fried to a golden brown, turn and fry the other side for a few seconds. Slide the crêpe onto a plate and continue frying, adding a little butter to the pan before each crêpe. When using the crêpes, remember that the presentation side is the first side fried; it is more evenly colored.

PASTRY

Makes 1¹/₂ pounds

4 cups flour
1 teaspoon salt
10 tablespoons butter, diced and chilled
2 eggs, chilled
6 to 8 tablespoons cold water

1. Put the flour, salt, and butter in the food processor. Use the on/off switch to cut the butter into fine pieces. If necessary, let the motor run for a few seconds to produce a mealy texture.

2. Beat the eggs with 2 tablespoons of water and, with the motor running, pour it into the bowl of the food processor. Add more water, 1 tablespoon at a time, until the dough begins to cohere. Stop the machine after each water addition, gather a little of the dough with your fingertips, and press it gently; if it sticks together, it is ready. Do not allow the dough to pull together into a ball; this overdevelops the gluten in the flour and toughens the pastry.

3. Gather the dough into a ball and transfer to a lightly floured pastry board. With the heel of your hand push small sections of dough away from you, pushing about 6 inches. Reassemble the dough and repeat one more time. Gather the dough into a ball, cover closely with plastic wrap, and chill for at least 1 hour. The pastry will keep in the refrigerator for several days.

ALTERNATIVE METHOD: Put the flour on a pastry board and make a well in the center. Into the well put the salt, eggs, butter warmed to room temperature, and 2 tablespoons of water. Mix the wet ingredients very well with your fingertips, then gradually incorporate the flour until the mixture becomes mealy. Add additional water, a little at a time, until the pastry holds together, then proceed with step 3 above.

NOTE: To prebake a pie shell, preheat the oven to 375

degrees. Roll out the dough, fit it into the pie dish, and flute the edges. Prick the bottom of the pie shell with a fork, fit a piece of parchment or wax paper over the pastry, and weight with dry beans, rice, marbles, or manufactured pie weights. Bake for 10 to 15 minutes or until the crust is firm, opaque, and lightly colored. To avoid a soggy bottom, remove the weights and paper from the pie dish, prick the bottom of the shell again, and return to the oven, with heat turned off, for about 5 minutes.

SOUR CREAM PASTRY

Makes 1 pound

2½ cups flour
salt
1 or 2 tablespoons sugar (optional, for a sweet pastry)
12 tablespoons butter, cut into pieces and chilled
1 egg
¼ cup sour cream

1. Put the flour, a large pinch of salt, and sugar, if using, into the bowl of a food processor; add the butter and use the on/off switch to chop the mixture into small, mealy pieces.

2. Beat the egg and sour cream together and, with the motor running, pour it into the processor. Process an extra second or so, but do not allow the pastry to pull into a ball or it will be tough.

3. Scrape the dough onto a lightly floured pastry board and knead for a minute or so. This pastry can be used immediately, closely wrapped and refrigerated for several days, or frozen.

ALTERNATIVE METHOD: To make the pastry in a bowl, cut the butter into the combined flour, salt, and optional sugar with 2 knives or a pastry cutter until the mixture has a coarse mealy texture. Beat the egg and sour cream together, pour into the bowl, and stir with a fork until the dough begins to pull together. Proceed with step 3 above.

GRAHAM CRACKER CRUST

Makes 1 9-inch pie shell

1½ cups graham cracker crumbs
¼ cup sugar
¼ cup melted butter

1. Combine all the ingredients. Press into the pie plate. If you find the crumbs sticking to your fingers, use a wad of plastic wrap for pressing. Chill to set the butter.

NOTE: Depending on the filling to be used with the shell, you might want to add a bit of cinnamon or nutmeg to the crumbs.

CRÈME ANGLAISE (LIGHT CUSTARD SAUCE)

The sauce will have a more satiny texture without the cornstarch, but with it, it will not curdle.

Makes about 2 cups

⅓ cup sugar
4 egg yolks
1 teaspoon cornstarch (optional)
1¾ cups milk
1 tablespoon vanilla, or a combination of vanilla and
    brandy, rum, orange liqueur, kirsch, or coffee

1. In a heat-resistant mixing bowl, beat the sugar and egg yolks together until they're pale yellow and when the whisk is lifted a ribbon can be traced on the mixture. Beat in the cornstarch, if using.
2. In a 1-quart saucepan, bring the milk just to the boiling

point. While whisking vigorously, pour the milk over the eggs in a very thin stream so that the yolks warm up slowly. Rinse out the pot to remove any clinging milk solids.

3. Pour the mixture back into the pot and set over medium heat. Stir with a wooden spatula or whisk until the sauce thickens; do not allow the sauce to reach the boiling point. This should take about 2 or 3 minutes; the temperature of the sauce without the cornstarch addition should be 165 degrees; and 170 degrees with it. Remove from the heat and beat for a minute or so, then add the flavoring. Cool, stirring often so that a crust does not form. Cover and chill.

RASPBERRY SAUCE

Makes about 1 cup

1 pint fresh raspberries or 1 10-ounce package frozen
   berries, defrosted
1 teaspoon orange liqueur
1 teaspoon lemon juice
½ cup sugar (only if using fresh raspberries)

1. Put the fresh or frozen berries in a blender or food processor and add the orange liqueur and lemon juice. Add the sugar only if using fresh berries. Blend to a puree, then strain to remove the seeds. Chill well.

CARAMEL SAUCE

Caramel Sauce will keep for months in the refrigerator in a covered container. Keep it on hand to enhance all sorts of desserts.

Makes 2 cups

2 cups sugar
½ cup cold water
1 cup warm water

1. Fill a mixing bowl with cold water and place it in the sink. Measure the sugar and cold water into a heavy saucepan large enough so that the sugar and water fill the pot only one-third full. (An unlined copper pot is the classic vessel, but an enameled cast-iron pot will work just as well. Do not use a lined copper pot because the intense heat will melt the lining.) Let the sugar-water stand for about 5 minutes, then cover pot and place on a very low flame to dissolve all the sugar crystals. When the mixture is clear, remove the cover and turn up the heat to medium.

2. Let the syrup boil briskly until it begins to color. Never stir at any point; the pot can be swirled, but stirring with a spoon will cause crystallization. It may take 5 to 6 minutes for the syrup to begin coloring. At this point it must be watched carefully or it will burn and take on a bitter flavor. As soon as the syrup turns a rich brown color, a minute or so after it begins to color, remove it from the heat and plunge the bottom of the pot into the bowl of cold water to arrest the cooking. Keep the pot in the water for about a minute, then add the warm water.

3. Return the pot to the heat and cook over medium heat to boil and dissolve the thick caramel. Scrape the bottom of the pot with a wooden spoon to incorporate all of the caramel into the sauce. Cool, transfer to a tightly closed container, and refrigerate.

NOTE: To give the pot a preliminary cleaning, simply fill it with water and boil to dissolve any trace of caramel clinging to it.

WHIPPED HONEY FROSTING

Makes 1½ cups, enough for a double-layer cake

½ cup honey
1 egg white
pinch of cream of tartar
⅛ teaspoon almond extract
⅛ teaspoon vanilla

1. Pour the honey into a small saucepan and place over low heat to liquefy. Meanwhile, beat the egg white in a bowl until foamy, add the cream of tartar, and whip until it forms soft peaks.
2. Slowly pour the hot honey over the egg white while continuing to beat, increasing the speed to high. Add the almond extract and vanilla and beat until the frosting is thick and fluffy.

CREAM CHEESE ICING

Makes about ¾ cup, enough for a single-layer cake

3 ounces cream cheese, at room temperature
2 tablespoons cream
1 teaspoon vanilla
½ teaspoon orange liqueur or orange juice
¾ cup confectioners' sugar

1. Place the cream cheese in a mixing bowl and use a wooden spatula to break it into pieces and begin softening it. Add the cream, vanilla, and orange flavoring and work another minute with the spatula. Switch to a whisk and beat the mixture thoroughly until light and fluffy.
2. Measure the confectioners' sugar into a sifter and gradu-

ally sift it into the cream cheese, beating well with each addition.

NOTE: Flavorings can be changed to suit the cake this icing garnishes. Rum, cinnamon, lemon rind, coffee extract, and chocolate are a few other possibilities.

THE COOKERY COLLECTION
From Pocket Books

___ **THE GOURMET GUIDE TO BEER** 46197/$5.95
Howard Hillman

___ **CROCKERY COOKERY** 47671/$3.50
Paula Franklin

___ **DIET SIMPLY . . . WITH SOUP** 46428/$4.95
Gail Becker, R.D.

___ **DR. MANDELL'S ALLERGY-FREE COOKBOOK**
49562/$3.50 Fran Gare Mandell

___ **FEARLESS COOKING AGAINST THE CLOCK**
47641/$3.95 Michele Evans

___ **FEARLESS COOKING FOR ONE** 49294/$4.95
Michele Evans

___ **KEEP IT SIMPLE (trade size)** 50736/$7.95
Marian Burros

___ **THE WAY OF HERBS** 46686/$4.95
Michael Tierra

___ **WOMAN'S DAY® BOOK OF BAKING** 46945/$2.95

___ **WOMAN'S DAY® COLLECTOR'S COOKBOOK**
46946/$2.95

___ **WOMAN'S DAY® BOOK OF NEW
MEXICAN COOKING (trade size)** 44672/$5.95

___ **WOMAN'S DAY® COMPLETE GUIDE TO
ENTERTAINING (trade size)** 44671/$5.95

POCKET BOOKS, Department CCC
1230 Avenue of the Americas, New York, N.Y. 10020

Please send me the books I have checked above. I am enclosing
$_____ (please add 75¢ to cover postage and handling for each order.
N.Y.S. and N.Y.C. residents please add appropriate sales tax). Send check
or money order—no cash or C.O.D.'s please. Allow up to six weeks for
delivery. For purchases over $10.00, you may use VISA: card number,
expiration date and customer signature must be included.

NAME _____

ADDRESS _____

CITY _____ STATE/ZIP _____

939

☐ Check here to receive your free Pocket Books order form.

Home delivery from Pocket Books

368